PASS
Interference

A HISTORY OF THE BLACK
QUARTERBACK IN THE NFL

WISDOM MARTIN

13TH & JOAN

For permission requests, write to the publisher, addressed "Attention: Permissions Coordinator," 205 N. Michigan Avenue, Suite #810, Chicago, IL 60601. 13th & Joan books may be purchased for educational, business or sales promotional use. For information, please email the Sales Department at sales@13thandjoan.com.

Printed in the U. S. A.

First Printing, March 2022.

Library of Congress Cataloging-in-Publication Data has been applied for.

Paperback ISBN: 978-1-953156-72-3
Hardcover ISBN: 978-1-953156-75-4

CONTENTS

INTRODUCTION

BY TRE' JOHNSON/ WASHINGTON FOOTBALL TEAM ALL-PRO OFFENSIVE LINEMAN

IN ALL MY LIFE EXPERIENCES THROUGHOUT MY 50 YEARS, NOTHING has brought together more people from different backgrounds, cultures, ethnicities, and socialization processes like athletics. I have seen sports break down social barriers and facilitate the integration of Black people into white America, even more so, or at least equal to that of civil rights pioneers like Martin Luther King Jr. I have argued that sporting events like the 1966 Citrus Bowl in which Morgan State Defeated Westchester, the USC Alabama game in 1970 when USC had several players of color on their roster and went onto rout Alabama on national television, and the 1966 NCAA men's division one basketball championship game in which Texas Western defeated Kentucky, compelled the majority culture in this country to become a little more open minded in terms of integration, or at least certain aspects of it. Yet, it is the sport that most defines the United States of America, this country's true national pastime in which the least amount of progress has been made Football.

It is scientifically proven that race is a social category and not a scientific one and cannot be found in nature. We as a species of Homo sapiens are more than 99% genetically identical, yet we still promote the concept of race and the limitations and discrimination that accompany it. A glaring example of this is seen in the treatment and experiences of the Black quarterback. The football world stigmatizes Black quarterbacks as inferior human beings and as a result of this stereotype, football has discriminated against and disenfranchised those who had the fortune, or misfortune depending on how you look at it, of playing this particular position. In essence, what the football world is saying is that, because of his melanated skin, the Black quarterback is less of a human being than his white counterparts. Indicating that he is a different species of human being entirely who should not be given the same consideration and opportunities as others playing this position.

The true tragedy here is that the people who do this just don't care about winning. Or instead, they'd rather lose their way than win using the best players available. I can say that what I have learned from my experiences is that football not only brought a tremendous amount of diversity to a common cause, creating allies out of people from varied backgrounds together, but it unified our purpose in that all of us wanted to win regardless of who was playing next to us. It only matters whether or not your brothers could get the job done...

ACKNOWLEDGEMENTS

I STARTED WORKING ON THIS BOOK COLLECTING DATA WITH MY father Wisdom D. Martin when I was a teenager. We had many deep conversations about race and professional sports. For that I am forever grateful.

I am deeply grateful and forever indebted to every single Black quarterback who played football on the college and pro levels who took the time to talk with me about their difficult journey. Each one of them, no matter how long or how often they played, is a pioneer. If they had not gone through the struggles, there wouldn't be Black starting quarterbacks or backup quarterbacks today. I also acknowledge their power, struggles, wherewithal, fortitude, insight, judgment, grace, and dignity. It is because of their endurance and profound qualities, abstract and concrete, that generations of quarterbacks who look like these brave men will feel the urge and the need to step in and step up to the role of quarterback. If you don't know where you have been, you can't know where you are going. It was extremely important to me that these men allowed me to tell their stories. Maybe one day there will be no conversations about quarterback skin color. Until then, knowledge is power.. All have been a valuable asset to make this project become a reality. You can be certain that this was a team effort.

FOREWORD

BY MIKE HILL /FOX SPORTS/BNC ANCHOR

WHEN YOU LOOK AT THE NFL ROSTERS OF TODAY, YOU'LL SEE strong representations of Black quarterbacks at the helm of teams. In fact you can argue that of the top 10 QBs in the league today, more than half of them are Black, including two who have been named MVP. However, before they overcame any hurdles, they had to break through barriers put up by NFL personnel, fans, and the media.

Obviously there is still a long way to go. Even though Black quarterbacks have made major strides, the playing field is still unequal when it comes to their white counterparts. They're still given more credit for their athletic prowess rather than their acumen,and while they may be given opportunities, their margin for error or criticism isn't the same.

As a sportscaster for over 25 years, I've seen first hand some of the obstacles and criticism they've had to overcome, and many of them have been tougher than any defense they've faced on the field. Wisdom does a great job taking you through these obstacles, abuse, and blatant discrimination Black quarterbacks have faced through personal stories from these players and others. I've known Wisdom for many years and I know how passionate he is about this topic and his mission to bring it to the forefront. *Pass Interference* does just that. I'm glad you're reading it because it's a topic we can't afford to take a knee on any longer.

"It was spoken, you don't play quarterback because you are Black."

— George Taliaferro
quarterback 1949-1955

CHAPTER 1:

QUARTER-BLACK OUT

To understand the problem of racism in professional football, we have to look at the time when the game began to grow. The roots of this American sport seeded in racism and discrimination that started on the field, continued on the sideline with the lack of black coaches and representation in front offices. That's where this country was when the game started. Blacks were not considered good enough, smart enough, capable of leadership simply because of their skin color. Since quarterback was the single most important position in football and the most high profile, team ownership did not want a black man to be the face of the franchise.

In pro football's early years, **Fritz Pollard (1920-26) and Bobby Marshall (1920-25) were** the first two black players. Pollard was also pro football's first black coach. Duke Slater (1922-31) was the first black offensive lineman. Those 3 players were pioneers for blacks in a game dominated by whites until the Great Depression that started in the 1930s. When the world economy crashed it caused the longest deepest depression of the 20th century. This is significant to this story because not only did blacks who were already suffering suffer more, but the jobs became harder to come by. Tensions between whites and blacks escalated. After hall of famer Duke Slater retired in 1931, blacks were shut out from football. There were no black players from 1934-1946. The football owners agreed to ban Black players from playing on any NFL team. This ban was pushed by Washington football team owner and known racist, George Preston Marshall. Marshall would end up being the last team to have a Black player in 1962 after the federal government threatened to revoke the team's stadium lease. After the NFL reintegrated in 1946 with Kenny Washington in Los Angeles, more racial problems would develop specifically around the most important position in the sport; quarterback. Owners wanted the quarterback to be the face of the franchise therefore blacks were not capable of leadership and not smart enough to be quarterbacks. The league would grow, the number of black players would grow. But the position of quarterback would continue to exclude and elude blacks decade after decade.

One of the first Black players to actually line up as quarterback was **George Taliaferro**. In 1949, he became the first Black player ever drafted by a National Football League team. During his college years at Indiana, Taliaferro had plenty of success playing several positions. He won football letters in 1945, 1947, and 1948. He is the only Hoosier football player to be named to All-America teams during three different seasons. As a freshman in 1945, he was first team all-Big Ten and led Indiana in rushing and punting. The Hoosiers were undefeated and won the Big Ten Championship. In 1948, he was first team All American and All Big 10. He led Indiana in passing, rushing, and punting. His impressive college resume was enough to get him drafted by a professional football team, but not as a quarterback. George Taliaferro was moved to running back.

On Wednesday January 10, 2001, I spoke with Taliaferro from his Bloomington, Indiana home. "The owners felt they had to respond to White America at large and not play a Black in the quarterback position. That's all it is," Taliaferro said. "There is no other reason."

Taliaferro spent his career playing all the skilled offensive positions: quarterback, wide receiver, running back, and punter. He started his career in 1949 with Los Angeles of the All-American Football Conference. In his first season, he played 11 games and completed 45 of 124 passes (36%) for 790 yards, four touchdowns, and 14 interceptions.

By the time pro football evolved into today's version of the National Football League, Taliaferro spent his first two years with the New York Yankees. In his first season he completed only three of seven passes for 83 yards and one touchdown in limited action as a quarterback. As a running back, he ran for 411 yards and caught 21 passes for 299 yards and five touchdowns. In 1951 he expanded his duties not only as a runner, passer, and catcher, but also as a punter. He punted 76 times for 2,881 yards. The next year at Dallas, again with a minimal role as a passer, he completed only 16 of 63 passes for 298 yards and two touchdowns. But it was his third year with Baltimore that was most significant. After injuries to Baltimore's starting quarterback and the two backups, the Colts coach asked him to fill in.

"There were no Black quarterbacks then," Taliaferro recalled. "My head coach in Baltimore was Keith Moesworth, a former Chicago Bear. We had three quarterbacks, Dick Flowers, Jack Del Bello, and Fred Ink. Fred got injured, Jack subbed in and got injured, and then Dick got injured. The coach asked me if I could play quarterback, and I said yes."

So, in 1953, Taliaferro started two games as quarterback for the Baltimore Colts.

"It was just another position to me. When I was in college, I played running back with passing options. I had played quarterback since I was eight years old because I could throw the ball. I didn't care about defense; I didn't care about reading defense. If you could run and get open, I could throw it to you. I knew every position and what everybody was supposed to do: the backfield, the line, and the receivers. But I never got the opportunity to play quarterback full-time."

Taliaferro said it became clear early on that the coaches did not want Blacks in charge of the offense on the field. "It was spoken, you don't play quarterback because you are Black," George said. "Web Eubank [coach] admitted that he would never consider me as a quarterback. I knew it was because I was Black. That's the only reason I didn't play. I'm not a big fan of Web Eubank. He admitted he should have played me as quarterback and built the team around me."

After making history as the first Black quarterback to start in the NFL, Taliaferro played the position sparingly for the rest of the year, completing only 15 of 55 passes for 211 yards and two touchdowns. He still carried his duties as a runner and receiver, and punted 65 times for 2,437 yards, but after that season in Baltimore, he would only throw two more passes over the next two years.

"There is still a double standard." Taliaferro's career included time with the New York Yankees, Dallas Texans [1952], Baltimore Colts, and he finished his career with Philadelphia Eagles. He retired in 1955 and returned to Indiana University to work as assistant to the president. In 1981, he was inducted into the College Football Hall of Fame.

The same year that George Taliaferro became the first Black to start a game as quarterback, Willie Thrower, backup to George Blanda, played quarterback on October 18, 1953 against San Francisco. At 5 foot 11, **Willie Thrower** had already made history in college as the first African-American to play quarterback at Michigan State. In the San Francisco game, Thrower completed three of eight passes (37%) for 27 yards and one interception. He never played the position again.

In 1955, a 16th round pick, **Charlie "Choo Choo" Brackins from Prairie View College**, played in his first game as a quarterback. Brackins played with the Green Bay Packers as a backup to starter Tobin Rote. The rosters had only 33 players back then, so Brackins also fielded kickoffs and was an emergency receiver. He became the third Black quarterback to play October 23, 1955 against the Cleveland Browns. Brackins saw limited playing time after the Browns were ahead 41-10. In the final two minutes of the game, Brackins threw two incomplete passes. It was his first and only game in pro football. Two weeks later, he was cut for breaking curfew. In 1960, he signed with the Dallas Texans, now the Kansas City Chiefs, as a defensive back. Unfortunately, a knee injury ended his career before he could play. After Charlie Brackins, it would be more than a decade before another Black quarterback would play in the National Football League.

The struggles of George Taliaferro, Willie Thrower, and Charlie Brackins would be indicative of the problems Black quarterbacks would face over the next five decades. With Brackins cut after one appearance and Taliaferro spending his final two years throwing only two incomplete passes, the Black quarterback disappeared from the NFL after the 1955 season.

That changed in 1968 when unfortunate circumstances opened the door for **Marlin "the magician" Briscoe** to quarterback the American Football League Denver Broncos. At the University of Nebraska-Omaha, Marlin Briscoe, who was 5'11", caught the eye of a Broncos scout who was actually looking at another potential draftee.

"Back in those days, of course, a Black quarterback was unheard of in the National Football League, and so society as a whole and the NFL community was just not ready for it. We were thrust into the position without warning. The eyes of the world were on me. If I had failed, then it would have probably taken a longer process for the quarterbacks that came after me," Briscoe says.

Denver drafted Briscoe in the 14th round to play both receiver and quarterback. "I negotiated my own contract. They told me I was good enough to play quarterback my first year. I agreed to play defensive back, but I wanted a three-day tryout at quarterback. They didn't want to do that, but they did it to appease me. Back then, they held open practice, and the media and the public could watch. I performed well and showed my talent." Briscoe actually started the season as cornerback, but a hamstring injury kept him off the field. He says after re-aggravating his hamstring in practice, coach Lou Saban met him in the locker room.

"I got to my locker and saw jersey number 15. I thought I was cut. That's the way they did things back then. If you came to your locker and your stuff was gone, you were cut. I turned and saw Coach Lou Saban. He said, 'My friend, you are now a quarterback.'" This was much to Briscoe's surprise. The deck was stacked against Marlin, the coach, and a winless Denver team with no offense and no quarterbacks.

Denver's starting quarterback, Steve Tensi, had broken his collarbone. The Broncos would go through several other quarterback injuries before settling on Briscoe.

"He [Coach Saban] didn't want to do it, but the owners at the time made him because we hadn't won a game. We had no points on offense, the other quarterbacks were hurt and others had been non-productive. So Saban basically had a gun to his head and was pressured by people who had seen me work out," said Briscoe. "It was a different style of ball. Steve Tensi, the starting quarterback, wasn't very mobile. The other quarterbacks started getting hurt."

With no other options, Briscoe would get his chance in the next game against New England at the end of the game after it was clear that Denver was not going to win.

"My first game against the Patriots, I got into the game with 9:49 left. We were down 20. My first pass was complete. We had an 80-yard drive that I finished with a 12-yard run. We eventually lost 20-17, but I performed!" Briscoe said. "I beat Bob Griese [Miami Hall of Fame quarterback] that year and had six touchdowns in two games. I was runner up for rookie of the year, but that was never publicized. Denver didn't get a lot of media coverage back then."

Briscoe started six games and played in 11 games over the course of the season. Marlin Briscoe was the first Black to play quarterback full-time in the NFL/AFL. In 1968, as Denver's quarterback in 11 games, Briscoe completed 93 of 224 passes (41%) for 1,589 yards, 14 touchdowns, and 13 interceptions. He also rushed 41 times for 308 yards and 3 touchdowns. He held the Broncos rookie record for total offense with 1,897 yards. At the time his 14 touchdown passes set a rookie record for Denver. Yet, after all that statistical success on a bad team, he says he was shocked by the team's next move.

"After the '68 season, I went back to Omaha [college] to get my degree. I only needed six hours. I had gotten calls from Denver saying Coach Lou Saban was having quarterback meetings and I wasn't invited. Yet I had ended the season as quarterback. The team had acquired quarterback Pete Lisk from the Canadian League. After I graduated, I went unannounced to the training facility. The secretary saw me and acted as if she had seen a ghost. She was evasive about the meetings. She didn't want me to catch them (Saban and the other quarterbacks) holding meetings. Eventually, they walked out of the quarterback meeting. I spoke to the other quarterbacks. Steve Tensi, who is a good friend of mine, said, 'I am sorry, man; I didn't have anything to do with this,'" Briscoe recalls. "Coach Saban didn't say anything. He just walked on by. It became evident that I wasn't going to get an opportunity to compete. In camp, Saban acted like I wasn't there. So I asked for a release."

Briscoe was confident that he had done enough as a rookie quarterback to get another quarterback job in the league.

"Saban said it would take a few days to release me. But he used those four days to blackball me from the league. When I was released, I got no calls. So I went home and was out of football."

With no interest, Briscoe ended up flying to Canada to play for the British Columbia Lions. "I went to one practice and didn't like Canadian football. I went back to the hotel and decided, 'I am not going to play quarterback in the NFL.' So I had to move to another position. Back then, Black quarterbacks were called athletes, not quarterbacks."

Briscoe was traded to Buffalo in 1969 where he would play until 1971. He says Buffalo coach John Rouse specifically told him he could play wide receiver but not quarterback. Another Black quarterback, James Harris (GRAMBLING STATE), was already on the Bills' roster backing up Jack Kemp and Tom Flores.

"Obviously, they were not going to have two Black quarterbacks in Buffalo. So I made the last cut in the last exhibition game. I played in practice as an emergency quarterback and had little time to play receiver."

He would only complete 4 of 9 passes over the rest of his career and never get the chance to play quarterback full-time again. He also didn't get to stay with the Bills long.

"After three years in Buffalo, it was time to renegotiate my contract. Guess who they hired? It was Lou Saban. They hired Lou Saban! He traded me to Miami."

Briscoe played for Miami from 1972 through 1974, then for San Diego and Detroit in 1975, and finally with New England in 1976. He was a receiver on the 1972 Miami team that went undefeated and won the Super Bowl. He caught 30 passes for the Dolphins in 1973 when they won the Super Bowl again. In 105 games, he completed 97 of 233 passes (41.6%) for 1,697 yards, threw 14 touchdowns, 14 interceptions. As a receiver, Briscoe caught 224 passes for 3,537 yards, and 30 touchdowns.

Briscoe now lives in Los Angeles where he teaches. Looking back over his career, he says he never had a problem with teammates or Denver fans when it came to him being the lone Black quarterback in the game. "The city embraced me. It was Lou Saban. I remember the first game I played in, Saban only gave me six plays. He had no intention for me to succeed. But I did. All the White players embraced me. He wanted me to fail so he could say, 'Now, look at him and shut up.'"

Briscoe says race was a big factor with Saban, and he was the only one in the organization that thought that way. "Saban used the excuse of my size instead of racism. I outperformed other quarterbacks. I didn't get my balls knocked down; I threw from the pocket, I scrambled. Basically, what they are doing now. There was no other reason why I didn't play quarterback, except for racism. People to this day don't know that the first Black center [Walter Highsmith] played the same day I started my first game. He played because Saban wanted a Black center for a Black quarterback."

Briscoe says he never got one negative comment or piece of mail from fans or the press about being a Black quarterback. "The fans actually helped me get through that." Now, he says things have changed and are much different than his 1968 season. He looks back on his career and considers himself one of the pioneers who opened doors for today's players.

"If I have a legacy and people saw the way I played, I showed that a Black man can think, throw, and lead. Black and White players rallied around me. That's what I am most proud of. African American quarterbacks are now looked at as quarterbacks. We have gone past that stage. Although I didn't get an opportunity the next year to compete for the position, four quarterbacks got drafted. Two played that position. I was proud of the fact that I had a hand in that. Had I failed, I don't think those quarterbacks would have gotten the opportunity. They were all 6'4", so the excuse they were too small couldn't be used. But they did use excuses like they threw too hard. We all had those struggles, but as a period of time has gone on, obviously a lot of those nay-sayers are gone."

The year Marlin Briscoe was drafted, Tennessee State quarterback Eldridge Dickey was the first Black athlete drafted as a quarterback in the first round of the NFL draft. Pro football Hall of Famer Ken Stabler was taken in the second round. The 6'2" Dickey was given an opportunity to play quarterback in his first two training camps, but never played the position in a regular season game. Stabler went on to have a great pro career. Dickey was moved to receiver and kick returner with Oakland from 1968-1971. In 1969, Dickey had a severe knee injury that cut his playing days short. He only played 18 games, catching five receptions for 112 yards and one touchdown.

On the college level, Wilmeth Sidat-Singh Syracuse played quarterback from 1937-1938. In those days, teams refused to play a team with a Black player. In 1937 Maryland refused, so Wilmoth had to sit out the game. Maryland won that game, but the next year in an October rematch, Sidat-Singh led Syracuse to a 53-0 win. He never got a chance to play in pro football.

From an NFL management standpoint, unless you were willing to switch to another position, the chance to play in the pros was almost nonexistent. For many years, coaches and owners would say Black quarterbacks in college had too much athletic ability to play one position.

Former NFL defensive back **Ken Riley** is one of countless quarterbacks who faced that dilemma coming out of college.

"It was a known fact that was what happened. **Eldridge Dickey,** who died not too long ago, from Tennessee State was a great quarterback. He was drafted number one by the Oakland Raiders. At the time, they drafted Ken Stabler and [Dickey]. He was switched to wide receiver," commented Hall of Fame defensive back Riley.

"There was Emmit Thomas. The list goes on and on, where guys were switched from quarterback to other positions-receiver or defensive back. It was a common practice."

Ken Riley had seen other Blacks change positions in order to get to the NFL. He was about to see it happen to him. When Riley was in college, there were 17 rounds in the NFL draft. He didn't think he would even get drafted. He was ready to do something else with his life.

"I didn't think I would get drafted. I was at a basketball game, and a guy came up to me and said, 'Cincinnati is on the phone.' They asked if I was interested in playing football. I was a good student. They said, 'We heard that you were going to engineering school.' At that time, people would try to get you for nothing like they are still doing with some of the athletes. What was probably going to happen was they were going to sign me as a free agent, but they said, 'Look, we are interested in drafting you in the next round.' They had just signed a guy out of Florida named Guy Denning, and they said, 'We are interested in signing you the next round, if you want to play.' I said, 'Yeah, I want to play.'"

The Cincinnati Bengals picked Riley in the sixth round.

"I was just so elated that somebody was even thinking about drafting me at the time. Especially a Black quarterback-that was unheard of."

Riley had played quarterback his whole life and never played another position. But the Bengals had other plans.

"When they signed me, that's what they had down there, the different positions I could possibly play. I was running a 4-4 forty. Most Black athletes, they were athletes. When I was drafted, you talked about 'slash.' That's what I was. It was Ken Riley the receiver-slash-running back-slash-defensive back. So I didn't know what I was going to play. Then when I went to the Bengals in 1969, Coach Brown said I was going to play defensive back. That's where I ended up."

Back then, very seldom did you hear about a Black center, quarterback, safety, middle linebacker, or free safety. Those were the positions that you didn't see many Blacks in.

"I don't know if you want to call it racism. We were not given the opportunity. I think there was a guy with Buffalo–James Harris," said Riley. "Then they had another guy out of Minnesota that didn't play. I thought I was a fair quarterback at the time. I had broken all the records at Florida A&M except one. I wasn't as tall as some of the guys, but I was an athlete. I could throw. I thought I was intelligent enough to learn the system. I didn't think that would be a problem. But we definitely were not given the opportunity."

Like a few others before him, he was not asked to play the position until after a series of injuries to the other quarterbacks. "At the time when we had some people hurt, he approached me about playing in that game. But at that time, we were playing the Steelers. That's when Hall of Famer 'Mean' Joe Greene was there. I was happy at my position. I didn't want to play quarterback then!" Riley joked. "At the time I was considered because we had so many people hurt."

Riley stayed at defensive back and never got to throw passes in the NFL. The switch worked out for Riley, who went on to have a Hall of Fame career as a defensive back. "Like I said, I started out in a position I never played before. I knew I didn't have any bad habits," remarked Riley.

Riley played from 1969-1983. He is fourth on the NFL all-time interception list with 65 interceptions. After his playing days, he was a Green Bay Packers' assistant coach from 1984-85, head coach of Florida A&M University from 1986-1993, and athletic director of Florida A&M.

Jimmy Raye (Michigan State 1965-1967) was considered one of the best college quarterbacks of his time. He led Michigan State to two Big Ten titles and a 1966 Rose Bowl appearance.

12

He also started in the "Battle of the Century" against Notre Dame in 1966 that resulted in a 10-10 tie. He was converted to a defensive back in the NFL. During his rookie year, Raye played defensive back for the Philadelphia Eagles.

Jimmy Jones (USC 1968-1972) as a sophomore in 1969 led USC to an undefeated season (10-0-1) and a Rose Bowl win over Michigan. He was the first Black quarterback to be on the cover of *Sports Illustrated* (9/29/69). In 1970 Jones was part of Southern Cal's all Black backfield, which was a first for any Division One major school. Jones led the team to a 42-21 win over all-White Alabama (coach Bear Bryant). It was a big event because the crushing defeat accelerated integration of all-White Alabama football. He had a record of 22-8-3 and at the time held records for career passing attempts, passes completed, attempts, passing yards, rushing attempts, career touchdown passes, single season passing yards, and touchdown passes. In the spring of 1972, no NFL team was interested in Jones as a quarterback. After a year away from football, he signed in Canada with Montreal. In 1974 he helped Montreal win the championship Grey Cup. It was his best season, with over 2000 passing yards, 18 touchdowns, and 577 rushing yards. Jones also played with Hamilton and finished his career in 1979 as a backup in Ottawa (backing up another Black quarterback Condrege Holloway).

In 1971, **Condrege Holloway (Tennessee) was drafted by the Montreal Expos**, but decided to go to the University of Tennessee. Holloway led the Volunteers to three bowl games. After a spectacular college career, the New England Patriots in the 11th round of the 1975 draft drafted him. But they wanted him to play another position. He opted for Canada where he played for 15 years. He captured the CFL championship in 1976 and 1983. His best seasons were the six years with Toronto

(1981-86). He threw for 16,619 yards and completed 1,149 passes and 98 touchdowns. In 1982, he had his finest season, throwing for 4,661 yards and 31 touchdowns. He later became assistant athletic director for football operations at Tennessee.

In 1972, the Buffalo Bills used their 10th round, 240th pick to select **Matthew Reed (Grambling State).** Standing at 6'5", he never played a round as a quarterback in a regular season game. He eventually played in the World League and Canadian League. "[Reed] was the best high school quarterback I had ever seen. He was a great player," said former Rams quarterback James Harris. "Had he come along now, a guy 6'5", 230 pounds in high school, running a 4-6, 50 touchdown passes as a junior, came back his senior year and ran 20. But they wanted him to play tight end."

Former NFL coach **Tony Dungy (University of Minnesota 1973-1976)** finished his career as the school's all-time leader in attempts, completions, passing yards, and touchdown passes. He finished fourth place in Big Ten history in total offense. Dungy was a two-time team Most Valuable Player, and played in the Hula Bowl, the East-West Shrine Game, and the Japan Bowl. In spite of his accomplishments, he didn't get drafted. Dungy eventually signed with Pittsburgh as a free agent safety in 1977. He also had the distinction of making and throwing an interception in the same 1977 game against the Houston Oilers.

Dennis Franklin (Michigan) was the sixth round, 144th pick of Detroit in 1975. As a quarterback at Michigan from 1972-74, Franklin played three years and led them to the Big 12 championship, and had a record of 27-1-2 as a starter. After joining the Detroit Lions, Franklin was moved to wide receiver. Franklin caught the first ever touchdown pass in the SilverDome. After a two-year career with the Lions, he worked in sales for WDIV television and later was a sportscaster for CBS. He later became a vice president of King World Productions in Manhattan before moving into other areas.

Cornelius Greene (Ohio State) 11th round, 318th pick of Dallas in 1976. Greene played on four Big 10 championship teams and four Rose Bowl teams. He had a 31-3-1 record and was MVP of the 1973 Rose Bowl. As a senior, he threw for 1,066 yards, completed 68 of 121 passes, and rushed for 518 yards.

"*I didn't want to make mistakes, didn't want it to be said that Blacks were not smart enough. With all the things going through your mind at the time, you felt you had to play perfectly without any mistakes, otherwise you would get cut.*"

— *James Harris*
quarterback 1969-1981

CHAPTER 2:

INCOMPLETE PASS

BY THE 1970S, BLACK QUARTERBACKS WERE STILL RARE. MARLIN Briscoe was shipped out of Denver to another team and put in another position. During this time period, **James Harris entered the league**. Harris had played for Grambling State University under legendary coach Eddie Robinson. He had all the impressive credentials of a college quarterback. He stood at 6'4" and 210 pounds. He played for a winning program with impressive statistics.

"I had a good career, and they had indicated that I would probably get drafted high," recalled Harris. "But what happened was during the draft, some teams called me and told me that if I switched positions, they would draft me earlier. At that time, I felt that they told me they were going to draft me as a quarterback. I decided quarterback was where I had the best opportunity to play. Coach Robinson had spent a lot of time working with me as a quarterback. He thought I could play. I told him that I wouldn't switch. True to their words, they didn't draft me the first day. I decided then that not getting drafted, realistically speaking, what chance did I have of playing? It didn't make any sense. I had basically said I wasn't going to play. Coach Robinson called me one day, and we talked about it."

Then on Day 2 of the 1969 draft, the Buffalo Bills picked Harris in the eighth round. "I got drafted the second day, during a time when there were no Black quarterbacks. Briscoe had played the year before, but they were not going to let him play again. Knowing that, knowing you get drafted like that, what chance do you have of playing? But Coach talked to me and said I definitely had the ability to play. If I didn't play, it would be that much longer before another guy got a chance to play. I decided to go ahead and play."

James Harris did play for the Buffalo Bills from 1969-1972 without any success. "That experience was different, coming out of the south and segregation, and going to Buffalo where I didn't know many people. I had to play quarterback knowing that one of the reasons Blacks weren't playing quarterback was because they were not smart enough. You can't make mistakes. When other guys went out, I had to stay in and study. I didn't want to make mistakes, didn't want it to be said that Blacks were not smart enough. With all the things going through your mind at the time, you felt you had to play perfect without any mistakes, otherwise you would get cut. Those were the conditions you played under."

Perhaps the most positive experience Harris gained from Buffalo was playing with former Black quarterback Marlin Briscoe.

"Marlin was my roommate. He had an experience in Denver. At that time, Marlin was not getting a chance to play. He was bitter. He thought nothing was going to be right or fair. He was a big help to me because he had been through it. Other guys on the team didn't understand him. I mean, everybody knows you're Black playing in those kinds of conditions, but at their positions, the best player plays. They didn't know what was going on with him inside. Marlin and I had a chance to talk about it."

At this point, James Harris and Joe Gilliam of Pittsburgh were the only two Black quarterbacks in the entire league. Marlin Briscoe felt a similar frustration. "Joe Gilliam felt it. The problem is a lot of times when we talked about that, the other players on the team would know what you were going through. But I don't think they understood the burden that you carried home with you inside." Harris spent most of his time in Buffalo as a backup. He was cut after the opening day of the 1972 season and went to work for the Department of Commerce. "They (Buffalo) cut me because they said they didn't want to have two young quarterbacks. We were struggling. Dennis Shaw was playing. The first game of the year, Dennis Shaw threw five interceptions. They didn't want two young quarterbacks, so they cut me." He admits he never thought he would play pro football again.

"There were no Blacks in the league playing quarterback, how could you ever think you would play? Think about it. What would make me think I would play quarterback when no other Blacks were playing? I had a rough time. I had hoped that I would get a chance. I drove from Buffalo to Washington, D.C., thinking about it. Realistically, this was it. Why would I have any reason to think that I would ever play again?"

Weeks passed and Harris had settled in with the Department of Commerce. He was also settling on the fact that he might not play again.

According to some publications, the late Rams owner Carroll Rosenbloom saw Harris when he was working with the Baltimore Colts front office. According to those reports, Rosenbloom wanted to trade for Harris, but the Buffalo Bills never called back. Harris got a second chance thanks to a fellow Grambling alum Tank Younger. At the time, Tank was a scout and assistant director of player personnel. "Tank Younger, who was a Grambling guy, worked for the Rams. Tank knew Grambling and Coach (Eddie) Robinson. He had seen me play a lot of times. He still had confidence in me and knew the Rams needed a quarterback for the practice squad. He told them about me. He went in and went to bat for me," Harris says. "When I got on the practice squad the first year, I traveled with the team and practiced every day. The following year, the Rams brought in a new coach, Chuck Knox. The next year, Coach Knox came in, and they traded for John Hadl. They drafted Ron Jaworski in the second round. Then I was one of the quarterbacks they didn't really know. In the pre-season, I got a chance to play and ended up backing up John Hadl."

John Hadl was league's MVP that year (1973). Once again, it did not look good for James Harris. In 1974, when the Rams struggled to a 3-2 record under Hadle, Harris replaced the league MVP. He started his fourth game in five years and completed 12 of 15 passes for 276 yards and three touchdowns in a 37-14 win over San Francisco.

A week after his first start, the team traded the 1973 Most Valuable Player and popular starter John Hadl to Green Bay. It was a trade that also brought all pro wide receiver Harold Jackson (Jackson State University) into view. Under Harris, the Rams went 7-2, and Harris completed 106 of 198 passes for 1,544 yards, 11 touchdowns, and six interceptions. "That year was different from Buffalo. I had matured some, was with a better team, and we were winning. Black people wherever you went showed their support. Supporters came wherever you were. That's one thing that was good about that time."

In 1974, Harris became the first Black quarterback named to the Pro Bowl and to win MVP. In the Pro Bowl game in Miami, Harris replaced an injured Jim Hart (St. Louis Cardinals) in the fourth quarter. The NFC trailed 10-3 until Harris tossed two touchdowns that were one minute and 24 seconds apart. The NFC won 17-10.

"That was a good feeling. The big thing was I just got an opportunity to play with good players. It was also a game where you didn't worry about being a Black quarterback." In the 1974 Pro Bowl season, he played 11 games and completed 106 of 198 passes (53%) for 1,544 yards, 11 touchdowns, and six interceptions. In the NFC divisional playoff game on December 22, 1974, Harris completed four of four passes for 60 yards and a 10-yard touchdown to tight end Bob Klein on the opening possession. The Rams went on to win 19-10 over Washington.

"There was a lot of fan support because we were winning, but also during that time, in spite of that, you continued to get hate mail, a lot of racial stuff. Drawing pictures of you, flushing you down toilets, all kinds of things. During that time, I was receiving death threats. I think it was America. You didn't have Black governors in leadership roles; it was a part of America. That position was kind of like that. People were not accustomed to seeing Blacks in that position, and that was part of the game. During that time, Coach Knox seemed to be receptive to my playing, that part was good. It wasn't anything noticeable with the players. Things in the media were sometimes slanted. For example, during the time I was training, I would throw the ball, and they would say I threw too hard. When the other guys threw their fast ball, they said they had great arms."

In the NFC championship game, Harris completed a 73-yard touchdown pass to Harold Jackson. But Harris threw an interception on the two-yard line that eventually led to a Minnesota Vikings score (14-3). In the fourth quarter, Harris tossed a 44-yard touchdown to Harold Jackson to cut the lead to 14-10, but the Vikings ran out the clock and went on to the Super Bowl.

The following year in 1975, Harris played 13 games and completed 157 of 285 passes for 2,148 yards, 14 touchdowns, and 15 interceptions. In the divisional playoff game on December 27, 1975, against the St. Louis Cardinals, Ron Jaworski had replaced Harris. The Rams won 35-13. In the NFC championship game on January 4, 1976, Harris was back at the helm as the Dallas Cowboys whipped the Rams 37-7.

Then, a career that looked to be on the rise fell off the map. In 1976, Harris spent most of his time on the bench behind Pat Haden and only played in seven games. "We had Ron Jaworski, Pat Haden, at one time they wanted Jaworski to play, and then Haden to play. That was a merry go round in itself."

Three years after being Pro Bowl MVP, Harris was traded to San Diego in 1977. It was the last season he would actually play in a regular season game. Harris played in nine games with the San Diego Chargers, completing 109 of 211 passes (51%) for 1,240 yards, five touchdowns, and 11 interceptions.

"When I first got there (San Diego), I started the first year, and then I got hurt. Dan Fouts came back and the next year they changed coaches. We both had pretty good pre-seasons, but he went in as number one and played well and ended up starting." With Dan Fouts running the show in San Diego, James Harris' playing days were done. He stayed with the Chargers until 1981 but didn't see any action.

"The big thing was, in college and high school, in order to play that position successfully, you have got to have confidence. You have to be able to go out there and show if you throw an interception, (you) go back out there and throw another one. That's the way you played in high school and college. But in pro ball, because of all the publicity around Blacks playing the position, it didn't allow you to do that. Every time they wrote about you in the paper, you weren't just a quarterback. You were a Black quarterback. You found yourself really concentrating on that, you found yourself trying not to make a mistake, and that affected your game. You never knew when you may not be starting anymore."

In 83 games, Harris completed 607 of 1,149 passes (52%) for 8,136 yards, 45 touchdowns, and 59 interceptions.

"I never thought about pioneering. When I was in college and high school, I worked at being good, better than anybody else. But when I was in the pros, my thoughts changed. It was more of the fact you thought about the reasons Blacks were not playing the position. The reasons were: not smart enough and too great of an athlete. I built my game around staying in the pocket. At the time when I was watching football, Johnny Unitas and Fran Tarkenton were pocket passers. They talked about how tough you were. When I was in high school, I studied football. Every Black quarterback that started running was a candidate to be moved to another position. So I built my game around what they did in the pros. When I came into the pros, my thoughts immediately were all those things. You spend your time concentrating on that. Holding the ball a little longer, not throwing the big interception that may get you benched, taking a sack here or there because you don't want to do nothing dumb or stupid. I looked at it from a standpoint of, maybe some of the things I did, if I didn't study and know what to do, then maybe the next guy's chances of coming in (would increase). They might say I didn't study. They didn't study. Those are the kind of thoughts I had," Harris says.

"If you ask people about me today, the ones who played with me, I bet most of them would say 'He had a great arm.' I could throw. I played in games with one leg, and couldn't even get back to the huddle. But nobody ever said I was tough. I played in championship games, but nobody ever referred to me as smart. Back then, the only description you could get was that you were big and you could throw. It wasn't blatant; it's those kinds of things that you see and you know. Those are the rules of the game, and you try to play according to those rules. It was obvious to me. It was never the fact Blacks couldn't play quarterback; it was the fact they were not ready for us to play. In the 1970s, I played in three or four championship games, led the NFC in passing, MVP of the Pro Bowl; based on that alone, that showed I could play. Yet later when Doug Williams came along, they were still saying 'Can Blacks play?' and they are still talking about it. Nobody was really ready to accept that."

During James Harris' early years in the league, **Joe Gilliam Jr.** started a brief and troubled career. Gilliam played at Tennessee State from 1968-1971. "Jefferson Street Joe" threw for 5,213 yards and completed 320 of 677 passes. As a senior in 1971, he threw a career high 25 touchdown passes.

"I go all the way back to 1972. I remember down in Southern University. His senior year," said Super Bowl MVP quarterback Doug Williams, "I went to the game because he was playing. I saw him do things in pre-game warm up: throw behind his back, spin it on his hand, hold it, and zip a pass. It was amazing. Nobody could do it like Joey," Williams recalled.

"He was a top-notch athlete who made my job easy because of his talent. He was smart, not just football smart. He knew the defense as well as any coach. That's what made it so easy. Coming in and watching him do the things he does on the football field, it was amazing," said former NFL player Robert Woods, who was Gilliam's offensive lineman at Tennessee State. Gilliam was drafted by the Pittsburgh Steelers as the 273rd pick in the 11th round in 1972.

Joe Gordon was the Steelers' public relations director the year Gilliam was drafted. "We had taken him in the 11th round of the draft that year. We already had two young, good quarterbacks–Terry Bradshaw and Terry Hanratty. The next day, out of curiosity, I asked Chuck Noll, our coach, why he would take another quarterback. He said that as the draft progressed, he could not believe that no other team had drafted Joe and it went from round to round. By the time we got to the 11th round I said, 'We are not going to get anybody nearly as good with nearly as much potential as Joe Gilliam.' So we selected him," said Gordon.

"I remember his first training camp; he was feeling his way. He was a little bit timid because it was a strange surrounding, somewhat of a hostile environment at that particular time in NFL history. So he was kind of feeling his way. Then the first day he went out on the practice field, it didn't take a coach long to realize why Chuck was so high on Joe Gilliam. The way he could throw the football was just incredible. He could throw from any position. He didn't have to be set. He could be moving left, he could be moving right, he was just incredible at that time."

In 1974, **Joe Gilliam became the first Black quarterback to start an opening day game in the NFL.** He completed 17 of 31 passes for 257 yards and two touchdowns in a 30-0 win over Baltimore. That performance earned him a spot on the cover of *Sports Illustrated* on September 23, 1974. He led the Steelers to a 4-1-1 record in 1974. His receivers included future Hall of Fame wide receivers Lynn Swann and John Stallworth, defensive stars "Mean" Joe Greene, Jack Lambert, Jack Hamm, Mel Blount, and running back Franco Harris. Gilliam completed 96 of 212 passes for 1,274 yards, 4 touchdowns, and 8 interceptions that year. His best game was against Denver in Week 2. He completed 31 of 50 passes for 348 yards, one touchdown, and two interceptions in an overtime tie (35-35). In Week 3, Gilliam was injured in a 17-0 loss to Oakland. Against the Raiders, he says he was banged up, but did not want to give the job back to Terry Bradshaw, who had been benched for Gilliam. So to ease the pain, Joe says, he started taking heroin.

His last start was in Game 6 against Cleveland where he connected on five of 18 passes for 78 yards. The Steelers won 20-16. The next week against the Falcons, Gilliam was benched and replaced by Terry Bradshaw.

"Back then, quarterbacks called their own plays. Gilliam wanted to throw. Coach Noll wanted to run with Franco Harris," said Joe Gordon. "Coach Noll made a change because he didn't feel he could win with a quarterback that, on third and inches, wanted to throw the ball. He thought we needed to be a little more conservative."

The Steelers had won two consecutive Super Bowls with Joe on the bench. By 1975, the drug problem had consumed Gilliam and he was out of the NFL, never to play again.

"I'm not sure whether that was the start of Joe's problems. I have my own theory," said Gordon. "It was frustration of losing the job, and in his mind, not really losing it on the field, but off field."

"Joe felt the game was a part of him. He could handle the game and was just as good as anybody," said former college teammate Robert Woods.

Former Steeler quarterback Kordell Stewart was a friend of Joe's, "Gilliam was one of the only Black quarterbacks before me that would play for the Pittsburgh Steelers. We had talked before we shut down the stadium (3 Rivers); that's kind of touching. He hung in there and supported me," said Stewart. "Knowing that he was a guy that paved the way for a guy like myself. It's a gratifying feeling to know that he was a pioneer at his time, but he just wasn't given the opportunity, or a chance, like he deserved. Mr. Gilliam was one of those guys who fought the fight."

Stewart said that on different occasions while he struggled on the football field, Gilliam offered him some sound advice. I had a chance to talk with Gilliam in Nashville in March of 2000 during the NCAA basketball tournament games.

"The racism that I experienced came from outside of the Steelers organization, from some of the fans. Coach Chuck Noll gave me a fair shot at the starting job," Gilliam told me a few months before he died. "Terry Bradshaw and I were good friends. People just were not ready for a Black quarterback at that time."

Joe Gilliam Jr. died on December 25, 2000 of a heart attack-just four days before his 50th birthday. In four seasons, he played in 20 games and completed 147 of 331 passes for 2103 yards, nine touchdowns, and 17 interceptions.

CHAPTER 2: INCOMPLETE PASS

"I guess I started this legacy of the Black quarterback being the first. Joe Gilliam, who was a contemporary, was a great quarterback who didn't get an opportunity to continue his assault on some of the records he would have broken. We all wanted to be here as a tribute to Joe's life. Not only his athletic life, but his life period," said former Denver quarterback Marlin Briscoe.

On December 31, 2000 during a Fox sports broadcast, Terry Bradshaw said that Joe Gilliam was one of his best friends on the team and that he was amazed at the way Joe Gilliam could throw the ball. He also said that, had he not had the problems he had with drugs, Terry Bradshaw would never have gotten to play. He also said that at the time, society was not ready to see Black quarterbacks.

"Joe Gilliam was the guy who paved the way for us. Without him, we wouldn't be here right now," says Atlanta Falcon Michael Vick. "I can honestly say that because of Joe Gilliam, I really didn't have as many obstacles that I had to overcome as he did. So, thank God we had somebody like him who was strong enough to fight through it and be successful. That's why we are here today."

"He is a great guy. He did a lot for guys like myself, giving us an opportunity that we have," said former Tampa Bay quarterback Shaun King.

Doug Williams says that in spite of his short career, there should be no confusion about Joe Gilliam's place in football history. "In my mind, every African American quarterback in the NFL should pay homage to Joe Gilliam. Joe Gilliam and James Harris made it easier for myself and the 20-some odd other quarterbacks that are in the league today."

Williams says there were still some problems with racism and attitudes toward Black quarterbacks, but nothing like what the people before him had to endure. "I was given an opportunity to be the man, where they had to earn every minute that they played. I can go back, reading some of the things that happened while he was there. But when you are 4-1-1, it's kind of hard to bench a guy who is 4-1-1. Joe had to deal with that, and that's a lot tougher than anybody can imagine."

Gilliam's father was also a bit of a pioneer. "I myself, years ago, was one who the door was closed to. So I could appreciate the fact that Joe did open one of those doors," said Joe Gilliam, Sr. "What we are talking about is a time in this country when there were doubts about whether or not a young Black athlete could lead on the highest level of football. Joe dispelled any doubts. This cannot be overlooked, because at the end of this, you see doors opened that were closed to young Black quarterbacks."

"The thing that people don't know about Joe Gilliam is that his father was the first Black quarterback in the Big 10. He was a reserve on Indiana's 1945 Big 10 championship team. He only played a series late in the 49-0 route. Then he went to the army," said George Taliaferro.

"There has always been a stereotype and stigma, you could say, that we had to be twice as good as the White quarterback before we could get the proper recognition."

— *Vince Evans*

quarterback 1977-1995

CHAPTER 3:

ROUGHING THE PASSER

BY THE MID '70S, JAMES HARRIS HAD BECOME THE ONLY somewhat successful Black quarterback in the NFL. That really wasn't saying much because he was the only starter for most of the decade. He led the league in passing in1976. He was the first black quarterback to start and win a playoff game. He was the 1974 Pro Bowl MVP and he led the LA Rams to the division title 2 straight years and back to back NFC Championships. Harris was the first black quarterback to start on opening day in the NFL. So you would think that his play on the field would have put to rest all the negative, racial stereotype actions about Black quarterbacks. After all, he had the statistics and a winning record that proved he was more than capable of doing the job. However, that didn't seem to have any impact on the negative stereotypes about the Black quarterback's abilities to lead a team. By the late '70s, the Black quarterback situation still had not changed. James Harris' career was winding down and he was relegated to a backup position in San Diego before he retired.

In 1975, New York Jets rookie **John "JJ" Jones** got his first and only start in the NFL. He started in place of Joe Namath in a Monday night game after Joe missed curfew.

Fisk was one of only three NCAA colleges in America that went undefeated and untied. "Seven NFL teams had inquired about me, but the coach kept the letters in his tabled desk, so that I would not be distracted during the '73 fall football season," Jones says. "So I did not know that Paul Brown (coach Cincinnati), nor Tom Landry (coach Dallas), nor five other NFL teams were interested in me. Oh well, it all worked for my good, because I did end up playing as the backup to 'Broadway' Joe Willie Namath."

In 1975, Jones came into the game for the first time in (Week 3, October 5) the Jets' crushing defeat by the New England Patriots 36-7. Jones completed 2 of 3 passes for 1 yard at the end of the game.

He started his first and only game (Week 10 November 23, 1975) on Monday night football due to an injury to Joe Namath. Jones completed 6 of 20 passes for 73 touchdowns and 2 interceptions. The Jets were crushed by the St. Louis Cardinals 37-6.

The previous week he came in at the end of the game against the Baltimore Colts (November 16) completing 6 of 15 passes for 86 yards, 1 touchdown, and 1 interception. The Colts destroyed the Jets 52-19.

Jones finished the season completing 16 of 57 passes with 1 touchdown, 5 interceptions, and 181 passing yards. Like many other Black quarterbacks during this era, he ended up playing in the Canadian football league.

"As far as my football career is concerned, I forfeited it when I shared with the New York media and the whole world the private words told to me by new Head Coach, Lou Holtz, that he had never had a Black quarterback play for him and that he never would," Jones says. "Jets Quarterback Coach Dan

Henning told me everything was going to work out for me if I did not say anything publicly about the action that Lou Holtz had taken against me. If I had heeded Dan's advice, I would have been the QB for the New York Giants instead of Joe Pisarchek, whom I replaced in Calgary, Alberta, Canada with the Calgary Stampeders Canadian Football League team."

Jones left New York City heading to the Calgary Stampeders Canadian Football League Team to replace their Quarterback Joe Pisarchek. "This happened just one week before General Manager Andy Robistelli of the New York Giants called for me to come play quarterback for him with the Giants. So you know the infamous history of that story of Joe 'P' and the Philadelphia Eagles' last play of the game fumble return for a touchdown that took Joe 'P' to Philly."

In his only season with the Jets, Jones played in 7 games, completed 16 of 57 passes for 181 yards, 1 touchdown, and 5 interceptions.

"In any case, my sports career reward can be summed up in a statement made by National Football League Hall of Fame Quarterback Warren Moon when he gave credit to former Los Angeles Rams quarterback 'James Harris and a couple of others' for his being able to play quarterback in the NFL. I met Warren Moon when he visited Mount Zion, my church home, in Seattle and I told him I was one of those 'couple of others'!" Jones recalled.

Jones also recalled quarterback 'Jefferson Street' Joe Gilliam from Tennessee State University. They were one of only three National Collegiate Athletic Association (NCAA) football teams in 1973 that went undefeated. The two schools were undefeated and on the same street less than a mile apart in Nashville, Tennessee. "I gave up my professional football career in the National Football League so that other African American quarterback/athletes that followed me from the likes of Doug Williams, Randall Cunningham, Rodney Peete to Vince Young and even Mike Vick could have a real chance to play QB in the NFL."

Tampa would eventually find some success with another Black quarterback from a historically Black college. Following in the footsteps of James Harris, **Doug Williams (Grambling State)** would become the next player to make an impact as a quarterback. After an outstanding high school career in Zachary, Louisiana, Williams played at Grambling State University. During his senior year in 1977, Doug completed 181 of 352 passes for 3,229 yards and 38 touchdowns. He set a Grambling record with 7 touchdowns against Langston. Grambling was 10-1 SWAC Champions. Doug finished fourth in the Heisman Trophy voting. Williams had an NCAA record at the time, 8,411 career yards passing. He had 93 touchdowns in his career at Grambling and won 35 of 40 games.

"You have to understand, I came out when owners, coaches, and general managers were afraid. They didn't want to take a chance on Black quarterbacks because they didn't feel like we were smart enough," Williams says.

He played for the Tampa Bay Buccaneers from 1977-1983. He made the all-rookie team in 1978 with 1,170 yards passing and 7 touchdowns as the Bucs went 5-11. In 1979, the team improved to 10-6 and made the playoffs. In the divisional game against the Eagles (December 29, 1979 in Tampa), Tampa led 17-10 when Williams iced the game with a 9-yard touchdown pass to tight end Jimmie Giles. Tampa won 24-17. In the NFC Championship game against the Rams (January 7, 1980), the offense disappeared, and Los Angeles advanced to the Super Bowl with a 9-0 victory (3 field goals). On January 16, 1980, Doug Williams set a Tampa record, passing for 486 yards in one game. The Bucs regressed however, finishing the season 5-10.

Doug's best numbers came in 1981, when the team was 9-7 and Williams completed 238 of 471 passes (50 percent) for

3,563 yards, 19 touchdowns, 14 interceptions, and 4 rushing touchdowns. But in the playoffs (January 2, 1982), the Dallas Cowboys crushed Tampa 38-0.

In 1982, the Bucs finished the strike-shortened season 5-4 as Doug completed 53% of his passes. In the postseason, Tampa led Dallas 17-16 after 3 quarters on a Doug Williams 49-yard pass to Gordon Jones. However, the Dallas Cowboys came back to eliminate Tampa 30-17 in the January 9, 1983 game.

In 1983, Williams' wife died of cancer and he was a "hold out" with the Bucs when they refused to pay him more money. Former Tampa coach John McKay once said that the worst mistake the organization made was not re-signing Doug Williams to a new contract.

After a bitter hold-out, Williams joined a new league called the United States Football League (USFL) and played for the Oklahoma Outlaws from 1983-85. There he threw for 6,757 yards and 36 touchdowns. Tampa Bay would not have another winning season until 1997. When the USFL folded in 1986, Williams returned to the NFL as a backup in Washington to Jay Schroeder. Washington coach Joe Gibbs had coached him as offensive coordinator in Tampa. In his first year back, he only threw one pass. At one point, Williams was almost traded to the Raiders, but Coach Gibbs changed his mind. During 1988, Williams became the starter until he got hurt and was replaced by Jay Schroeder. Eventually Coach Joe Gibbs would bench Schroeder and turn to Doug Williams for the rest of the season. He played 11 games, completed 213 of 380 passes (56%) for 2,609 yards, 15 touchdowns, and had 12 interceptions, but Williams would make his biggest impact in the postseason.

During the playoffs, Williams led Washington to a 17-10 victory over the Minnesota Vikings in the conference title game (January 17, 1988). He tossed a 42-yard touchdown to Kelvin Bryant and the game winning 7-yard pass to Gary Clark in the fourth quarter to secure a trip to the Super Bowl.

In Super Bowl 22, Doug Williams completed 18 of 29 passes for 340 yards and 4 touchdowns as Washington blasted Denver 42-10. It was one of the biggest upsets in football history because John Elway and the Denver Broncos were so heavily favored.

One of those touchdowns was to **Gary Clark,** who recalls playing with Williams during that magical playoff run.

"Honestly you can't ask for a better role model than Doug Williams. He's a patriot of the game of football and life in general. What he did in his career as a Black quarterback in the NFL is unbelievable. I owe my first Super Bowl to Doug Williams. He made my dream come true. My touchdown in the Super Bowl came from Doug Williams; honestly he was supposed to take a blitz read but he gave some ground and was able to throw the ball to me," says Clark. "Doug Williams and what he was able to accomplish, the way he goes about his life, and the way he mentors individuals is something that people never even hear about. He's a true patriot to the game."

Clark says the pressure of being a Black quarterback in that Super Bowl was brought to him. At the end of the day, he was just trying to win the football game.

"The amount of pressure he was under, I could not believe. I would not want to be in his place and have the additional pressure of being the first Black quarterback to have an opportunity to win a Super Bowl and to come through and do it the way that he did it in style. Eighteen plays of magic, a good percentage of that was because of Doug Williams."

Clark says it completely changed the narrative. Before then, typically, when Black quarterbacks came into the league, they got moved to receiver, running back, or defensive back. They weren't able to play the position they were gifted at playing.

"Doug Williams was just a beast! It's just a privilege to be in his presence. Every time I see him, he knows this. I kneel down and kiss his feet. He's like a god to me. He is literally a football god," Clark says.

"To me, he (Doug Williams) put to rest a lot of questions. There are still people who say that was just a fluke. But he beat their White god. He beat Elway. That is no fluke. That was as paramount as Jesse Owens winning the Olympics," says Mike Williams, Doug's younger brother, who was also a quarterback at Grambling State.

"When you are a Black quarterback in the NFL, I don't care what anybody else says, you are the one wearing the shoes. It's tougher to think. The good part about it is, I think we have gotten to the stage where we have gotten new ownership and new coaches with different ideas. A lot of the coaches are young enough to have gone to school with Black players. They understand that they [Black quarterbacks] are a lot smarter than they gave us credit for back in the day, and I don't think today it's about color at that position, as much as it is about playing the guy who is going to get the job done. That's the good part about it," Mike says.

Unfortunately, this NFL rags to riches story didn't have a happy ending as far as pro football goes. In 1989, Washington fluttered early and Williams was benched after only four games. The next year he was released from the team and his NFL career ended.

Vince Evans (USC) had attended Ben Smith High in North Carolina before making the decision to head West for college. "It was interesting," Evans said. "I came out of Greensboro, North Carolina with a dream of making something out of my life. I had inquiries from other schools back in that area, but I thought that for me to be able to play quarterback I needed the visibility of an institution like Southern Cal. So I came out West with a dream and went to a junior college for one year, then transferred to Southern Cal. After my first year there I met a guy named Pat Haden who became sort of my mentor. He was a senior. I had a chance to play behind him. I think in the history of the school, it probably had two African American quarterbacks prior to me being there. Willie Wood was one and Jimmy Jones was the other. So it had not been a school heavy in African American participation at that position. But Coach John Robinson saw a lot of potential in me. I was thinking that maybe I should consider changing positions because the likelihood of me making it in the NFL as a Black quarterback was somewhat small. But to Coach Robinson's disagreement, he thought that I had all the skills to make it happen there. He brought in a quarterback guru, if you will, by the name of Paul Hackett who had been with Cal Berkley and had produced standouts like Steve Bartkowski and Joe Roth. He came down to give me skill sets, the tutelage of playing the quarterback position."

But even with playing out West, Evans couldn't escape the racism that was directed towards an African American who simply wanted to play a certain position in the game of football.

"In my senior year, we lost our first game and Coach Robinson had gotten some mail saying, 'What are you playing that nigger for?' In their mind, I should not have even been a backup. In my junior year, we were 8-4 and that was considered a losing season by Southern Cal standards. I got mail and bumper stickers. They created 'Save USC football,' and 'Shoot Vince Evans.' I remember one time, we were getting ready to play UCLA and I got some mail that said, 'Nigger, if you go out there on that field, I am going to blow your brains out.' So I took the letter to Coach Robinson to let him check it out. He called the LAPD and showed it to them. They had extra manpower at that particular game. It was challenging, but yet, I was just so into competing and winning, the tradition of the school. While I was not totally oblivious to the racial undertones that took place, I would say my enthusiasm for playing the game and the camaraderie of my teammates was the overwhelming perspective that I had."

In 1976, Vince's senior year, he completed 95 of 177 passes (54%) for 1440 yards, 10 touchdowns, and 6 interceptions in

12 games. Evans then turned his attention to the pros and to becoming a quarterback in the NFL.

"I had some indication that I was going to get drafted. I had talked to a number of different scouts, and they indicated that I would go higher in the draft if I would have been selected to play another position, like running back or defensive back. I was such a good athlete in their minds, that I could make it at either one of those positions. So my thought was, if I was such a good athlete, why not use those skills at the quarterback position and excel?"

Evans was eventually taken in the 6th round by the Chicago Bears. Before he would throw his first pass in the league, he had taken up another position to prove himself.

"Me not wanting anybody to give me anything, I was there to contribute. I wanted to gain the respect of my teammates. I came into the league having to measure up to, or at least, be on the same field as Walter Payton. To be around that kind of greatness, you just don't want to sit around and collect a check. At least that wasn't my mentality. I figured, 'Hey, I am going to get out here and show these guys that I am a part of the deal.' But after I got blasted one time and got the wind knocked out of me, I told the coach, 'I think I need to stick to quarterback.'"

Evans went on to play several years with the Bears under Mike Ditka. "It was good. He [Ditka] had a lot of respect for me and I certainly had a lot of respect for him. He was a guy that basically let you know up front what he was thinking. I always appreciated that in people."

At one point during the early years of Vince Evans and Doug Williams, they were the only two Black quarterbacks in the league. Evans says a double standard was a big reason that Black quarterbacks were not common.

"There has always been a stereotype and stigma, you could say, that we had to be twice as good as the White quarterback before we could get the proper recognition. If we did something on the same level as our White counterparts, there was nothing said about that. So that inherently was noticed by the team, and other players would look at you. There was an underlying feeling that you couldn't make mistakes. If you made mistakes, you were probably going to get criticized by the coach and probably get taken out of the game. And it puts a lot of unnecessary pressure on the position. You felt like you had to basically go and be Superman out there."

When the Bears drafted Jim McMahon as a top quarterback out of BYU, Evans' days as a starter in the windy city appeared to be numbered. Then a start-up football league called the United States Football League (USFL) began play. They started plucking big-name players from the NFL and high-profile players from the college ranks, like Steve Young (BYU), Heisman Trophy winner Herschel Walker (GA), Heisman Trophy winner Mike Rozier (Nebraska), and Heisman Trophy winner Doug Flutie (BC). They attracted them with the guarantee of lots of money. They also lured several veteran players with some lucrative offers. Vince Evans was one of those players.

"I think he [Ditka] was a little disenchanted with me, by virtue of the fact that I had another offer from the USFL and decided to go that route and take the so-called guaranteed money. I did what I thought was proper for my family and I left the Bears after the 1983 season."

Life in the USFL with the Chicago Blitz and Denver Gold was much different than playing in the National Football League. "It was a learning experience. It was something that I thought I was good enough to be a starter in the league. So when that opportunity presented itself in the USFL, I took it and ran with it and had the opportunity to play on a regular basis. It was a new league. I was getting used to a bunch of new players and whatnot and I think it would have succeeded, but the financial structure of the league was its downfall," Evans says. "I am grateful for the experience. The financial structure wasn't backed by Lloyd's of London. Once you got that check, you definitely wanted to go in a hurry and make sure it wasn't going to bounce on you."

Thanks to bad financial moves, the league folded, but Evans still wanted to play football. So he tried to get back into the NFL.

"I still had a strong desire to make a contribution to the league. I contacted several teams. I contacted the Broncos and a number of different teams just wanting to have an opportunity to get back into the league. I contacted the Raiders and they said they weren't really interested but to check back with them. Then they had the NFL strike. They had the replacement games. I came in and worked out. They said, 'Yeah, you are good enough to play for us but there is no guarantee after this is over that we will keep you because we got Marc Wilson,' and Jim Plunkett was still there. So I played well and made some impressions and they kept me and this fellow named Eddie Anderson who was a free safety, and I remained with the organization for another 10 years."

Evans says he also got a chance to play for the first Black coach in the modern era, Art Shell.

"It was awesome playing for Art, you know that he was a player's coach. He had been in the trenches. He knows how the players think. We wanted to win for Art because he made us feel like we were a team. I look back on that as one of the highlights of my career. I put Art in the same category as Jackie Robinson. There would have never been a Jackie Robinson (first Black player in baseball) if there hadn't been Branch Rickey (LA Dodgers GM who signed Jackie). So kudos have to go out to Al Davis (Raiders owner) for being that guy that says, 'Hey I am going to take the stand and say, 'I believe in this guy who has been in my organization for 15 plus years as a player and I'm going to give him the opportunity to lead.'

"Marvin Lewis. What more do you have to do to prove that you are capable? This guy took an expansion team and obviously, its defense was the hallmark of the team. And he is up as a top candidate to get the job, and he is shined over. His time will come. There is no doubt about that. But it doesn't take very much to see that we get looked over quite handily when it comes to coaching jobs."

During the years Vince Evans played pro football, there were not many other Black quarterbacks playing the position. So he says bonding with the few that were in the league was important. "There was like this unspoken bond that we had between one another. It didn't have to be a lot of words shared because the experience was similar. How do you go about taking a team to the Super Bowl and being the MVP and can't get a gig the next year? Those are the kinds of things we all have in common, and how we have been looked upon to do the supernatural events on a game-by-game basis. There is an unspoken bond and respect that I have for all those guys."

Vince Evans spent his first year as a kick returner with Chicago (13 returns for 253 yards/19.5 average). In 1978, he only threw three passes and completed one. In 1979, he played as a backup, throwing for 608 yards and 4 touchdowns. He became a starter with a bad Chicago Bears team in 1980 and 1981. His first year as a starter with the Bears in 1980, Vince played 13 games, completing 148 of 278 passes (53%) for 2,039 yards, 11 touchdown passes, with 8 touchdowns rushing, as the Bears went 7-9. He tossed an 89-yard completion, which was the longest at Soldier Field at the time since the club had moved from Wrigley Field for the 1971 season. On December 7, 1980, Vince led the Bears to a stunning 61-7 victory over the Green Bay Packers at Soldier Field. Evans completed 20 of 24 passes for 316 yards. It was the most by a Bears quarterback in 10 years. In 1981, the Bears were 6-10, but Evans put up his best passing numbers, completing 195 of 436 passes for 2,354 yards and 11 touchdowns. By 1982, the 3-6 Bears had other plans that didn't include Evans. Brigham Young's second year player, Jim McMahon, would eventually take the job. By 1983, Evans played for the United States Football League's Chicago Blitz until they folded after three years. He signed on with the Oakland Raiders during the 1987 strike season for a few games. When the strike ended, he was kept as a backup. From 1987-95, Evans filled in considerably as a backup with the Raiders. During his last season with the Raiders, in 1995, he played 9 games, completed 100 of 175 passes (57.1%) for 1,236 yards, 6 touchdowns, and had 8 interceptions.

Starting for the injured Jeff Hostetler in 1995, Evans threw scoring passes of 73 and 46 yards to Raghib Ismail as Oakland went 6-2. That same year, while with the Oakland Raiders, 40-year-old Vince Evans was 23 of 35 passes for 335 yards.

Vince Evans' career numbers include 100 games. He completed 704 of 1,390 passes (50.6 percent) for 9,485 yards, 52 touchdowns, and 74 interceptions. He retired at age 41.

Looking back over his career, Evans didn't really burn up the record books, yet he still played an important role in the future of the Black quarterback.

"My whole career was more of a testimonial than it was statistical. I was all about going in and trying to make a situation better as a result of me being there. Whether that was bringing the team back from a deficit or encouraging a guy to give it his best. Whether it was Bo Jackson, Marcus Allen, Tim Brown, I just felt like whether I was number three on the depth chart or I was number one, you were going to get every ounce out of Vince Evans' body in terms of physical capabilities and spirit."

Evans does think however, that racism was a major factor when it came to coaches and owners dealing with Black quarterbacks. "I think it's like anything else. When people don't know they are afraid, they are unsure; they are reluctant to take a risk. Once something has been proven, once Doug Williams broke the threshold and took them all the way to the big dance and won in grand fashion, now that opened up a whole new sphere of influence for the African American quarterback," said Evans. "Now I think it's in vogue. Teams are starting to recognize that if given the ample opportunity to compete, then the Black quarterback can do the job as good as anybody." Evans says the fruits of the labor of the quarterbacks of the past are now appearing in the form of today's mobile quarterbacks. "If it were not for the Jimmy Joneses (USC) and the Marlin Briscoes, the James Harrises and the Joe Gilliams of the world, who knows where we would be? I take my hat off to Warren Moon and Doug Williams. Those guys really paved the way for the modern Black quarterbacks of today. It's definitely taken too long. There have been other competent, qualified quarterbacks. Had they been given the opportunity to go through that maturation period, then there is no doubt that they would have had the ability to lead and perform with their teams."

Currently Evans is in the real estate development business, finding raw land to build industrial business parks for major companies.

Vince Evans' progression and acceptance in the NFL was slow, but there were some quarterbacks who had to wait years before getting an opportunity just to be a backup.

Warren Moon (University of Washington) is another Black quarterback who exemplified the struggles of trying to get the opportunity to play in the NFL.

Warren was all city and all state in high school, but the major colleges wanted him to switch to another position and play receiver. Moon refused and decided to go to a junior college. After two years at West Los Angeles Community College, he landed at the University of Washington. At 6'2", Moon was the Pac-8 Player of the Year and Rose Bowl MVP as a senior. That year he completed 56% of his passes and threw 11 touchdowns. In 1977, he led the Washington Huskies to the

Rose Bowl (for the first time since 1963) to a 27-20 upset of Michigan. During his three years as a starter, Moon completed 242 of 496 passes for 3,277 yards with 19 touchdowns. He would later be inducted into the Husky Hall of Fame (1984) and into the Rose Bowl Hall of Fame (1997). He was one of the top quarterbacks in college. A proven winner. But he did not get a single invite to the NFL draft combine. He says he didn't even get a private workout with a team. This caused him to be bitter, because in his mind, his own country didn't want him, but Canada did.

"There were a lot of people in the NFL who didn't think we could lead a team and be the face of a franchise," Moon says. "We were not good enough for the thinking positions, we were good enough to be athletic, to run, jump, and block."

Moon, like many other successful Black college quarterbacks, went to play in the Canadian League with the Edmonton Eskimos. Over the next six years, Moon would become a football legend. From 1978-1982, he led Edmonton to five consecutive Grey Cups (Canadian championship). Moon also rewrote the Canadian football record book. He started 41 of 96 regular season games he played in. He passed for 21,228 yards, completed 1,369 of 2,832, and tossed 144 touchdowns and 77 interceptions. He played in 10 post season games with 138 completions on 257 attempts, 2,353 yards, 12 touchdowns, and 7 interceptions.

In one season he threw for 5000 yards in 1982. The next year he threw for 5,648 yards.

NFL teams finally came calling. Oakland. Seattle. Los Angeles. Houston Oilers. Moon chose to sign with Houston because of his relationship with Oilers Assistant Coach Hugh Campbell, whom he worked with in Edmonton.

Moon eventually got to the NFL and became one of the most prolific passers in league history, but he had to go through it to get to it.

When he got to Houston, the team was 3-13 his first year, and Moon was the highest paid player in the NFL. The fans were abusive and racist toward him, saying things like, "Warren, you're chunking that ball like you're chunking a watermelon." He had to explain to his son why a fan in the stands yelled out loud, "I can't believe they gave that f******N****r 14 million dollars."

Moon says he, like many other Black quarterbacks, played with the weight of representing his race and representing his teams.

He played for Houston (84-93), Minnesota (94-94), Seattle (97-98), and Kansas City (99-2001).

Here is an overview of Moon's career.

"The game is a much more wide-open game than it was when I was playing. It was more run dominated, run oriented when I was a player. They didn't throw the ball as much as they do now.

Quarterbacks are throwing the ball for 4500-5000 yards every year. Back when I played, if you threw for 4000 yards that was a big season. The game has opened up, and I think that's what everybody wants. They want to see the ball in the air, and they want to see more scoring. The running game is still important, but running backs are being used in a lot of different ways. They are catching a lot of passes out of the backfield," Moon says.

In 205 games of the NFL regular season, Moon completed 3,972 of 6,786 passes. He also rushed 541 times for 1,734 yards and 22 touchdowns. He accounted for 50,937 yards of total offense.

Moon held the league record for quarterbacks with eight straight nominations to the AFC-NFC Pro Bowl ('88-95). He played in his ninth Pro Bowl in 1997. Moon retired at the end of the year in 2001.

"I played against Moon and he was very smart and very accurate. He threw one of the prettiest passes by a quarterback," says former NFL cornerback John Booty (Jets, Eagles, Cardinals,

Giants). " Back in the day the quarterback was considered a thinking man's position. Teams didn't think Black players were smart enough to handle it and plus it was leadership of the team. They wanted a White player to lead," Booty recalls.

One year after Warren Moon entered the NFL, **Randall Cunningham, standing at 6'4",** was the second round 37th pick of the Philadelphia Eagles. The UNLV star was the first quarterback taken in the 1985 draft. Cunningham was the third quarterback (following John Elway and Doug Flutie) in NCAA history to throw for over 2,500 yards in three straight seasons. Cunningham holds the UNLV passing records in career completion percentage (57.9%), completions (614), yards (8,290), and touchdown passes (60). In addition to being a fantastic quarterback, Randall averaged 45.6 yards per punt during his collegiate career. He was All-Conference as a quarterback and punter for two straight years.

In **1989,** he was the first quarterback to lead his team in rushing for three straight seasons. He set Philadelphia's single-game record for passing yards (447). He threw a career high five touchdown passes as the Eagles erased a 20-point deficit to beat Washington. **Cunningham kicked a 91-yard punt against the Giants, which was the third longest punt in NFL history. In 1992, Cunningham** led NFL quarterbacks in rushing (549 yards). He became the NFL's all-time leading rusher among quarterbacks, but the Eagles sputtered again in the postseason, losing to Dallas in the divisional playoffs.

By 1994, it was the beginning of the end for Cunningham in Philadelphia. Ray Rhodes became Philadelphia's coach and Cunningham was eventually benched and replaced by Rodney Peete. The Eagles finished with a 10-6 record. Cunningham's biggest highlight of the season was **an 80-yard punt** at Dallas. It was the second longest of his career and third longest in team history. In **1995,** his last year in Philadelphia, Cunningham started the first four games. He completed 69 of 121 passes for 605 yards and three touchdowns. At the end of the season, he was released. In **1996,** Cunningham did not play. In **1997,** Cunningham returned to the NFL after signing a free agent offer with Minnesota. He punted the first two games of the season in place of injured punter, Mitch Berger. He took over for an injured quarterback, Brad Johnson, in December and would not give up the starting job. Cunningham rushed for 71 yards against Detroit, threw four touchdown passes against Indianapolis, and led a fourth quarter comeback win over the NY Giants in the wildcard playoff game in **1998.**

After taking the job from an injured Brad Johnson, Cunningham had a career year with the Vikings; he led them to a 15-1 record. He had a career high 34 touchdown passes. He threw for 3,704 yards and completed 60% of his passes. He broke the team record of 33 touchdowns set by Warren Moon, but the high-powered offense that had shocked the entire league vanished down in the conference championship game. The Vikings lost to Atlanta.

In 1999, Minnesota was predicted to once again be strong contenders for the Super Bowl. However, the team struggled from the opening game and after six weeks they had a record of two wins and three losses. After six weeks Cunningham led the league in passing by completing 124 of 200 passes (62%) for 1,475 yards, 8 touchdowns, and 9 interceptions. But the team was 2-3. As a result, Coach Dennis Green benched Cunningham in Week 6 at half-time because the team only had 85 yards total offense. With Jeff George at the helm, the team scored three touchdowns in the second half, but still lost the game 2-4. Cunningham was buried on the bench and would never throw another pass with Minnesota. The team finished 10-6 and made the playoffs. But they were blasted by eventual Super Bowl champion St. Louis Rams.

In 2000, Cunningham refused to take a pay cut to stay with the Vikings so he was released June 1. He signed with the Dallas

Cowboys as a backup for Troy Aikman. In his first game of the season, Cunningham completed 13 of 26 passes for 135 yards and 1 interception. He replaced an injured Troy Aikman, who was 0 for 5 with 1 interception. Dallas lost to the Eagles 41-14.

The next game, Week 2, he started against Arizona. In the first half, he completed 12 of 12 passes for 140 yards and 2 touchdowns. He led the team to a 21-13 halftime lead. However, the Cowboys lost the game by one point. Cunningham completed 24 of 34 for 264 yards, 3 touchdowns, and no interceptions.

In Week 3, he started against Washington, filling in for an injured Troy Aikman. He led the cowboys to their first win, completing 10 of 23 passes for 188 yards, 2 touchdowns, and 1 interception. In the 27-21 win, he tossed a 79-yard touchdown pass to Chris Warren after he fumbled the snap. "That's why we got him. We felt he could play for us if Troy was hurt," said Dallas head Coach Dave Campo. "The thing he did was move around and make plays with his legs."

Randall also tossed a 16-yard pass to tight end Jackie Harris to put Dallas ahead for good.

In Week 4, Cunningham was back on the bench and replaced by Troy Aikman. The Cowboys lost 41-24.

Cunningham returned in Week 10 against Philly and completed 14 of 22 passes for 109 yards in a 16-13 loss. In the game, Randall suffered a groin injury that sidelined him for the rest of the year. He had completed 74 of 125 passes for 849 yards (59%), 6 touchdowns, and 4 interceptions.

In 2001, Cunningham signed as a free agent backup with the Baltimore Ravens. It was his final season in the league before retiring in the summer of **2002.**

"After Doug Williams, Warren Moon, and Randall Cunningham, it showed they were capable enough to know the complications of the playbook and make plays that opened doors," says defensive back John Booty, who played with Cunningham and against Moon. "It was great to watch Randall use his athleticism to make plays when the defense thought they had him. He used his legs to make plays, and he had an accurate and strong arm."

While Moon and Cunningham made a name for themselves in the league, **Rodney Peete (USC)** was also trying to find his niche in the pros. In 1989, Rodney was the 6th round, 141st pick of the Detroit Lions. Peete had been a first-team All-American and an All-Pac 10 Conference player. He left USC as the all-time leader in pass attempts (1,081), completions (630), and passing yardage (8,225). In addition to being a quarterback, he was sensational on the baseball diamond too. He was an All-Pac 10 3rd baseman for the Trojan baseball team in 1988, when he hit .338 with 12 home runs and had 46 RBIs. In the 13th round of the 1989 amateur draft, he was also drafted by the Oakland A's. He opted to play football instead.

He had a long career as a backup after leaving Detroit. He played games in Dallas, Philadelphia, Washington, Oakland, and Carolina.

Johnnie Walton (Elizabeth City State) was drafted in 1969. He was on the LA Rams practice team for three years but never played during the regular season. He went back to Elizabeth City State (NC) as a physical education instructor. In 1974 he signed with Chicago and San Antonio in the World League. Finally, he got his chance in 1976 after joining the Philadelphia Eagles as a backup to Roman Gabriel. He completed 31 of 65 for 338 yards, 3 touchdowns, and 3 interceptions in 4 seasons. Walton's most productive season as a backup was his last season in 1979. He played in eight games, completing 19 of 36 (52%) for 213 yards and 3 touchdowns with 1 interception. From 1979 to 1983, Walton returned to coach at Elizabeth City State. Then it was back to football in 1983 as quarterback for the new pro football league, the USFL (United States Football League). He became the starter for the Boston Breakers, then eventually the team's QB coach. Over his career, Walton played in 15 games, completed 31 of 65 (47%) for 333 yards, and had 3 touchdowns and 3 interceptions. In 1986, he returned again to Elizabeth City State as the assistant vice chancellor of development. By 1989, Walton was coaching at his alma mater. He later became athletic director and football coach at Elizabeth City Middle School.

Dave Mays (Texas Southern University) played three seasons in the league with Cleveland and Buffalo *(12 games completed 80-156 for 937 yards, 7 touchdowns, and 11 interceptions)*. His career as a backup ended in 1979.

In 1976, the expansion Tampa Bay Bucs drafted **Parnell Dickinson (Mississippi Valley State)** in the seventh round. Dickinson was a backup for Heisman winner Steve Spurrier. The team was dreadful and finished 0-14. Dickinson got his first and only start against Miami. He completed his first four passes before getting hurt. He missed the remainder of the season, and his playing days were pretty much over. In his rookie season, Number 18 played in 8 games and completed 15 of 29 passes for 210 yards, 1 touchdown, and 5 interceptions. In 1977, he was cut and resigned during mid-season, then cut again at the end of the year.

"I won every award except the Heisman. I won all these awards, led the nation in passing, and didn't get drafted until the sixth round. If I were a White guy and did all those things, would it be the same?"

— Don McPherson
quarterback 1988-1990

CHAPTER 4:

MOVING THE GOAL LINE; OH CANADA

THE STATS DIDN'T SEEM TO MATTER. WINNING DIDN'T SEEM TO BE enough. Size only mattered depending on who you were. The teams kept moving the goal line, therefore denying lots of capable successful college quarterbacks. When the NFL teams consistently rejected their quarterback skills some players decided it was better to go play in the Canadian Football League where there had always been plenty of chances to play.. The grass was greener for Black quarterbacks, even though the money, exposure, popularity, and level of competition were not even close to American football.

The best Canadian league quarterback in history, Black or White, was Warren Moon. In spite of his accomplishments, the NFL scouts decided to pass on him. He made the decision to play in the Canadian League with the Edmonton Eskimos. Over the next six years, Moon would become a football legend. From 1978-1982, he led Edmonton to five consecutive Grey Cups

(Canadian championship). Moon also rewrote the Canadian football record book. He started 41 of 96 regular season games he played in. He passed for 21,228 yards, completed 1,369 of 2,832, and tossed 144 touchdowns and 77 interceptions. He played in 10 post season games with 138 completions on 257 attempts, 2,353 yards, 12 touchdowns, and 7 interceptions. Moon eventually got to the NFL and became one of the most prolific passers in league history. He played for Houston (84-93), Minnesota (94-94), Seattle (97-98), and Kansas City (99-2001).

It's a pattern that started decades earlier. In the '60s, a multisport athlete named Sandy Stevens exploded onto the college football scene. Stephens led Minnesota to the national football title in 1960 and the Rose Bowl the following year. That year, the six-foot 215-pound player became the first Black All-American quarterback. He was selected in the second round of the 1962 draft by the Cleveland Browns and in the fifth round by the New York Jets. But he never played quarterback in the NFL. He did spend a short time with Montreal. Stevens later got into banking, real estate, and social work. He was also a broadcast analyst for the Gophers.

In the '80s, Syracuse quarterback **Don McPherson** was one of the more notable Canadian stories. As a senior, the All-American was the most efficient passer in the nation with 2,341 yards, 22 touchdowns, and 11 interceptions. During his career, he had helped turn a 3-6-2 team into a national contender with an unbeaten regular season. He finished second in the Heisman voting to Tim Brown of Notre Dame. He had passing records, the awards, an undefeated season, and the national championship game. But in the 1989 draft, NFL teams were not impressed.

"There was no mood, if you could imagine what that's like. How much attention is given to the process today? There was virtually no attention at all. Paul Hackett was with Dallas at the time. He was the quarterback coach. He came through

Syracuse and worked me out. Dennis Green was in San Francisco, he came in and worked me out. But both of those workouts came fairly late in the process. Other than the two of them, there wasn't as much as a phone call for me," Don recounts. "I led the nation in passing over Troy Aikman [Dallas Cowboys], which is a curious thing. But the whole thing about being labeled as a runner was not because of what I did, but what I could do."

The NFL scouts had stereotyped McPherson as they had so many other quarterbacks before him. They claimed McPherson was too short at 6'1". They told him he was an option quarterback and not the prototype drop-back passer who could sit in the pocket. They said he didn't have the arm strength for the pros. McPherson was eventually drafted in the sixth round with the 149th pick in the 1989 draft.

"I look at it this way, If I were a White guy who went from 5-6 to an undefeated season, it would have been a different story. I won every award except the Heisman. I won all these awards, led the nation in passing, and didn't get drafted until the sixth round. If I were a White guy and did all those things, would it be the same? Then you can look at a guy like Danny Wuerfell. Here is a guy who I think a lot of people were curious as to why he didn't go as high, but the difference is how many opportunities did he get after he was there?"

McPherson made the team as a backup. It looked like a good situation to grow and develop. He would sit on the bench behind another Black quarterback, Randall Cunningham.

"I was there with Randall. It was interesting. I felt that I was in a good situation, not because I was there with Randall, but because of Doug Scoville, who was really the guy who changed Randall's game. Randall came in with what Randall would call a 'nasty throwing motion.' And Doug Scoville really changed the way Randall was releasing the ball. Doug was the quarterback coach at BYU for so many years when Jim McMahon was there and Gifford Neilson. Then he went to San Diego State. Doug knew about the forward pass. I felt that was a good situation. With regard to being on the team, things were very good. As far as the rest of the league, I knew for me it was Philadelphia or nothing." At first, there didn't seem to be any issues in Philly. "With Randall being the number one guy, no. The interesting thing about being a backup, people love you a lot better than the starter."

While McPherson got extended playing time in the preseason and did what he thought was a good enough performance to at least be the number two quarterback, the coaches never played him in a regular season game.

"If he had gone in the sixth round because people said his arm was not strong enough, or he didn't throw a drop back game, fine. I will go in the sixth round, but give me the opportunity to show myself. When I played in Philadelphia in the preseason games, I played the whole game against the Cleveland Browns, and won the game throwing two touchdowns. Every opportunity I got to show what I could do throwing the football, I did well. Well enough to win the opportunity to continue to do it. But in my case, if I didn't win there, if I didn't turn it out, I was done. That was true of a lot of Black quarterbacks at that time."

So after a short stint on the Eagles bench and no playing time, it was decision time for McPherson.

"After two years of being on the roster, I told Buddy Ryan, 'Listen, I am the number three guy. I am going to be number two next year. Matt Cavanaugh can't last that much longer.'

"Buddy was in my corner and they had no intention of getting rid of me. I went back to school to finish up my degree and then Rich Kotite [new coach] came in. Kotite and I had been friends prior to this; he came in as quarterback coach. I decided to come back during the off-season to not only learn his system but to help with the language and everything. I came back from mini-camp and got word they were talking to Jim McMahon."

Veteran McMahon had led the Chicago Bears to the 1985 Super Bowl, but his skills had since diminished. He eventually fell out of favor with Coach Mike Ditka and was released.

"That was the same year that I met Warren Moon down in Houston, as a matter of fact. I was in Houston with Warren in a bar and on the screen was a picture of an Eagles helmet and McMahon. So I told Warren, 'I guess they are trying to make a move and get me out of there.' Literally, that's how I found out they were talking to McMahon. I went back to camp and of course, I wasn't signed. It was a voluntary camp, and I told Kotite in the middle of practice, 'The minute you give McMahon one of my reps, I will compete with him.' He was an old man. If you give him my reps, you are giving him my job. And you are not allowing me to compete. You're telling me he needs reps because he is new? The minute they did, I walked out. I still didn't have a contract. It's bad enough I am competing against a guy who won a Super Bowl. Now you are going to take some reps from me. So I left. In the process of that happening, Warren Moon told me Cody Carlson [his backup] was upset in Houston, and he wanted out, so Warren talked with the Oilers and the Oilers came and offered Mike Rozier for me."

Rozier was a 1,000-yard back for Houston who had won the Heisman trophy at Nebraska. In 1990, McPherson was traded, but he landed in another bad situation.

"Buddy said no initially. But when I walked out of camp and didn't want to come back, they eventually traded me. When I went to Houston, they used me to get Cody Carlson back into camp. It was another ugly situation. I only lasted a few weeks in Houston. I walked out and literally threw the uniform at the general manager [Mike Holovak]."

By 1991, McPherson was back in Philadelphia with the Eagles. It turned out that the opportunity to play still was not there.

"Kotite was the coach. Kotite and I were friends; he brought me back up. I resigned during the off-season and they drafted Casey Weldon [Florida State]. He couldn't play, and they brought in some guy named Brad Goebel who played at Rice; he was horrible. They cut me for him. So that's why I went to Canada. I said the hell with y'all."

Fed up with being ignored and not given the opportunity in the NFL, McPherson decided to do something he vowed he would never do. He was like other Black quarterbacks who had not been given even the slightest chance to succeed. He went to the Canadian football league.

"I swore I would never go to Canada to play because I felt like I was better than most of the guys in the NFL. And it was more of, 'If y'all aren't going to let me play here, I am not going to play.' I wasn't that in love with the game of football. I am not that in love with football that I want to leave the country. When I eventually did go, it was because I really wasn't ready to stop playing. But I was not of the mindset to deal with the bull-s**t of the NFL."

McPherson spent the next 3½ years in Canada with Hamilton and Ottawa.

"I was more interested in the sociology of playing in Canada than anything else. To see which American players ended up there and to look at how much they put in. The attitude about football wasn't the same as it is here. It still isn't in Canadian culture. That to me, was more interesting than the game."

But being a Canadian league football player was much different than being in the NFL in America. McPherson described it as miserable.

"It was reminiscent of some of those movies you see about minor league baseball. It was a trip."

At this point, McPherson says he was playing football in Canada as more of a case study than anything else. He looked at the social aspect of the players that were there as opposed to being in America. One thing it didn't take long for him to figure out was that racism was definitely a factor that kept him from succeeding in the NFL.

Since McPherson's playing days at Syracuse, several other players have gotten the chance to follow in his footsteps. Marvin Graves was a record-setting passer at the school who played in Canada. Donavan McNabb, who also left his name all over the Syracuse record book, was a first-round draft pick in the NFL. They both walked in through the doors that Don McPherson had opened for them, yet he doesn't consider himself a pioneer.

"People say that to me at times. I don't consider myself to be a pioneer as much as one of those guys who was on the trail who didn't die, jump off, or stop. Because to me, the pioneers were the **Joe Gilliams**, and even guys like **Willie Totten at Mississippi Valley State**. Even though Willie didn't get a real shot, Willie put up some numbers. And that started to change the attitude. You have to look at guys in some of the major colleges who just put up some numbers and made people believe it could happen. Those are the guys, to me, who are the pioneers. Those are the guys. I got booed in the Carrier Dome. But nobody called me a 'nigger' in the Carrier Dome. They got it in places. To me, the pioneers are the guys like Doug Williams, who is on the field down in Tampa trying to lead his team and you got people who are supposedly his fans calling him a 'nigger.'"

After his football days, Don started several community outreach programs and continued to teach at Adelphi University in Garden City, New York. The Brooklyn native also kicked off a broadcast career from 1996-1998 with WBZ Radio (Boston) as co-host of Sports Sunday. In 1999 and 2000, McPherson was a sideline reporter for ESPN college football and commentator for NBC sports in 2001.

But at least Don McPherson got drafted. At least he made the team as a quarterback.

Another mind-boggling story of how the NFL ignored Black quarterbacks was when one of the most prolific, record-setting passers in football history never got the chance to play. **Mississippi Valley State's Willie "Satellite" Totten** passed for 61 touchdowns in 1984. He is the quarterback who tossed passes to NFL hall of Famer **Jerry Rice** in college.

"I used to always look at the San Diego Chargers," said Totten. "The way they used to throw the football. I look at it in terms of I want that to be me throwing that ball. But back then, White quarterbacks were the only role models. You didn't have many Blacks. You had Doug Williams, who was struggling to try to stay in the league. You had Randall Cunningham, the one who everybody had high hopes on. Then you had Warren Moon, just getting into the league from Canada. Then you go back. You had James 'Shack' Harris and Joe Gilliam that played in Pittsburgh. Those guys played before my time. I really didn't relate to those guys like I did with Doug Williams and Warren Moon and Randall Cunningham."

Totten played at Mississippi Valley State from 1982-85. Totten threw for 12,685 yards, 139 touchdowns, and averaged 317 yards. In 1984 he completed 324 of 518 passes (63%) and 56 touchdowns. "All the scouts were telling me there was no way, you were projected anywhere from the third to the sixth round."

Yet, in spite of all his accomplishments, he was never drafted.

"I was devastated. You go there and you know that you have set records, done something no other quarterback has done in the history of the game in college football, and then you get the opportunity. [You] feel that you have done all that you can do as a college player. Then no one gives you a shot. The thing about it is, we had scouts there every day working me up until the combine. I look back on it and try to find out what happened. All the team doctors check you out. In 1983, I had a torn ACL. I didn't know about it. As a player, I wasn't paying that much attention. They said, 'I don't think his knee would hold up through training camp.' Each team I went to, three or four doctors would examine me. I think back then, all of them failed me during my physical.

The only team that showed interest in Totten was Oakland, but by the time they called, he had made other plans.

"The Raiders did call. They called to give me a free agent shot. But I had already signed with British Columbia in the Canadian league. At the time, I was upset. I was just going somewhere where somebody wanted me. At least they drafted me in the territorial draft. They were going to wait until after the draft. At that time you had 12 rounds. Then after that, they called me asking me about being a free agent. I would have been satisfied if I had been taken in the last round; it's just like a free agent. To call me to give me a free agent shot–I was kind of devastated."

The 6'2" gunslinger who had once thrown for 599 yards in a college game decided to play in Canada. He spent three years in British Columbia and Toronto.

"Canada is something different, playing on the big field. Guys moving, guys running around at will. It was different, I must admit. In terms of the style of play, you throw every down. That's something that I did in college. It was making an adjustment to the different hash marks, the long end zones, and the wide field."

Totten got his only opportunity in the NFL during the strike year of 1987, but he says it wasn't much of an opportunity. On October 4, 1987 against the Indianapolis Colts, Totten fumbled five times. The next week, he fumbled four times against the Patriots.

"At the time, I came over from Toronto. You could still see the opportunity wasn't there in terms of giving fair shots, a person going through five centers during the time of five weeks. Every week you are playing with a different center. Then getting the opportunity to really go out and show yourself, you could see the attitude of the coaches. They were still waiting, hoping it was going to be over any day. I think they were putting up a front like they were doing their job, but I don't think they really concentrated on anybody there unless the person stood out.But it was an experience that gave me an opportunity to go there and see how that level is played. To be in that type of atmosphere was great for me. It was an opportunity to show what I could do."

While Totten enjoyed his playing days in Canada, he says the only reason he didn't get a real chance in the NFL was because of his skin color and the coaches' attitudes about Black quarterbacks.

"I think racism had a lot to do with it. At the time when I came out, there were a lot of questions. 'How could he do that? I can't believe he put up those numbers!' It was even stated one time in the sports information office that they didn't know how to keep stats. It's no way a person could throw that many yards. No way could a person catch that many passes. I think instead of just giving me credit for what I did on the field, they didn't want to do that because it was unheard of. You look at the league. At the time, you had only three Black quarterbacks: Cunningham, Moon, and Doug Williams. Now, 15 years later, you got Black quarterbacks all over the league, even in starting roles.

"I think it's gotten a lot better, but we still have a long way to go. You have many more Black quarterbacks getting the opportunity to at least show what they do. At one time, that was unheard of. You had to be a special type of person to get that opportunity. The same thing happened with Warren Moon. He spent five or six years in Canada before he could prove that he could play. But now it's a lot better. You have a lot of guys who are third string quarterbacks, even backups."

Totten has put behind him the playing days of the pros and turned his attention to college. He went on to become an assistant football coach at his alma mater, and in 2002, was named the head coach at Mississippi Valley State.

"Overall, I felt I got a bum deal. Life goes on. And so far, I am doing what I want to do, and that's coaching. I can let the guys know some of my experiences so they can be able to relate. Football is not for everybody. You have to be able to make the best out of the opportunity. You have to have a Plan B. That Plan B is to go on and be successful in life."

Grambling quarterback Mike Williams wanted to follow in the footsteps of his older brother Doug Williams. As a senior in 1980, he had also set several records at Grambling and anxiously awaited a phone call from an NFL team on draft day. He got that call from the Oakland Raiders.

"They called me the day of the draft and told me they were definitely going to draft me in the fifth round, and it never happened."

Williams says they even sent him a plane ticket after the call. He says he never got an explanation as to why he wasn't picked.

"They did say they wanted to bring me in as a walk-on, but by that time, Ottawa had given me a guaranteed contract. I wasn't going to pass with one bird in the hand and one in the bush. Naturally it was devastating [for them] to tell me they were going to draft me and nothing happened. So I just took the contract and went to Canada and played football."

While it was a chance to play the position in the pros, life in Canada was not like the NFL. "Canada is a whole different type of atmosphere, as far as the athletes are concerned. It's professional football but it's about three or four steps above the highest level of college football. It's nothing like the NFL. It is professional football, nonetheless. It's a different kind of game. I think 80% of the NFL players could not play in the Canadian Football League simply because it's a different kind of football game. Really, it's a quarterback's haven, because you really get to express yourself as a quarterback."

During his days in Canada, he played on several teams, including Edmonton, where a record-setting Black quarterback named Warren Moon was rewriting the record books. "I played with Warren Moon and, I tell you, of all my football careers, the one guy that I respect the most is probably Warren Moon. Warren and I played together for a couple of years in Canada and I was kind of under his wings. I will be eternally grateful for everything Warren has done for me. It was awesome. Everybody wants to play but sometimes you just want to watch him play. He was a class act. The consummate professional at what he did. It's a shame the guy isn't more well-known in the circle of being what he is."

Williams played 4½ years in the Canadian Football League with Montreal, Toronto, Edmonton, and British Columbia. "Canada is a very mobile game; it's constantly moving. You've got to be able to cover a lot of territory with the field being the size that it is."

Williams never got a chance to play in the NFL. He says racism was one of the reasons why. "I think it had a lot to do with it. It also had to do with the fact that I came from a small college–Grambling in Louisiana. And I wasn't the towering 6'4", 225-pound quarterback. I was right at six feet. So that made a difference. For me, being Black, I wasn't the typical Black quarterback at that time like James Harris, Doug Williams, and Joe Gilliam. But it had a lot to do with the fact I was Black. Anybody who says it didn't–they can look at themselves in the mirror and say, 'I am lying'. That's what it was."

He also thinks that the league used double standards when it came to Black and White quarterbacks. "I look at the fact that Pat Haden played for the Rams; there is no way this guy, or even Doug Flutie, for that matter, would have gotten an opportunity to play. There is not a Black quarterback anywhere near their height that would have gotten an opportunity to play in the NFL. Doug Flutie got in on a 'Hail Mary' pass, let's face it. Pat Haden got in because he was a Rhodes Scholar. It had nothing to do with ability; it had to do with skin color and who you are going to give an opportunity to. The guys that are getting those opportunities that Doug Williams and James Harris had - a role was laid out for them. Don't take it for granted; don't all of a sudden forget where you came from. Just as quickly as you got there, it can turn around on you. I think the young kids today tend to forget the struggle of Doug Williams, James Harris, and Joe Gilliam."

Here are some of the other Black quarterbacks who had to go to Canada after a successful college career:

In 1987, **Georgia Southern quarterback Tracy Hamm** was the 6th round pick of the LA Rams as a running back. The 5'10", 190-pound passer opted for the Canadian league (1987-1999) and never played in the NFL. Hamm had an MVP season (1989) throwing for over 4,000 yards and rushing for over 1,000 yards. He led Edmonton to the championship in 1990 throwing for 36 touchdowns, rushing for 1096 yards. He also led Canadian team Baltimore to the championship in 1995.

In 1981, quarterback **J.C. Watts of Oklahoma** went to consecutive Orange Bowl wins and MVP honors in 1980 and 1981. He was the eighth round, 213th pick by the New York Jets. Instead of playing running back like the Jets wanted, he decided to play quarterback in Canada. Watts signed as a free agent with the CFL Ottawa Roughriders. He played in Canada from 1981-1986 with Ottawa and Toronto. He was the MVP of the 1981 championship game as a rookie. After his football days, he ventured into the world of politics. Watts is currently a Republican congressman representing Norman, Oklahoma.

In 1981, **Tennessee State's Joe "747" Adams** was a 12th round selection of the San Francisco 49ers. Adams never threw a pass in the NFL. He joined the Canadian League team in Saskatchewan. During what was his best year in Canada, he threw for 3,312 yards and 19 interceptions.

In 1982, **Tennessee State's Brian Ramson** signed as a free agent with the Houston Oilers. He would back up Warren

Moon from 1983-1985, but he never threw a pass in the NFL. He eventually played in Canada with Montreal.

In 1985, **Tennessee State's Gilbert Renfroe** signed as a free agent with the Atlanta Falcons. Renfroe passed for over 8,000 yards and 43 touchdowns in four seasons in Canada with Ottawa and Toronto. He was cut and re-signed four times from the Atlanta Falcons in 1990. In February of 1990, he was signed to a two-year deal with Atlanta. He never threw a pass in the NFL.

In 1993, **Syracuse quarterback Marvin Graves** had been a three-year starter in college. He was the 1990 Aloha Bowl Most Outstanding Player, the 1992 Hall of Fame Bowl MVP, and the 1993 Fiesta Bowl Offensive Player of the Game. Graves held Syracuse passing records for career yards (8,466). No NFL team picked him in the 1994 draft. He was drafted by the CFL's Toronto Argonauts. Graves played with Toronto, Hamilton, and Montreal from 1994-1997.

In **1989, Terrence Jones of Tulane** was a seventh round, 195th pick of San Diego, but he never threw a pass in the NFL. In 1986 as a sophomore, in the season opener, he set a school record passing for 388 yards. He finished the year with 2,124 yards, completing 159 of 284 passes with only seven interceptions. In 1987, he became Tulane's career total offense leader. Jones led Tulane to Independence Bowl losses to Washington. He completed 17 of 40 passes for 248 yards, one touchdown, and 91 yards rushing. As a senior in 1988, Jones had career total yards of 9,445 yards. He ranked, at the time, in the Top 10 in NCAA history. He led the team in rushing and passing and at the time held all of Tulane's passing records.

Wayne Johnson (6'4") of Georgia was the 11th round 296th pick by Indianapolis in 1989. But he never threw a pass in the NFL.

In 1989, Steve Taylor of Nebraska was the 12th round, 323rd pick by Indianapolis. He ended up playing in the

Canadian league. He never threw a pass in the NFL. The Fresno, California native played from 1985-1988. He is in the Nebraska Hall of Fame.

Fred McNair of Alcorn State signed as a free agent with Dallas in 1989. The original "Air McNair" lost his senior year of eligibility at Alcorn over a grade controversy. He missed all NFL combines and workouts. McNair signed with the Dallas Cowboys practice team, but never threw a pass in the NFL. He was released in 1990 and signed with Canadian league's Toronto in 1991. He later played in the Arena League with the Florida Bobcats. In 2000, he was traded to the Carolina Cobras.

Reggie Slack of Auburn was the 12th round, 321st pick of the Houston Oilers in 1990. He never threw a pass in the NFL. He was released in August that same year. He joined a practice team in October. In 1992, he joined the World League New York/New Jersey Knights, the Canadian league's Winnipeg team in 1992, Toronto in 1993, Hamilton in 1994, Birmingham Barracudas in 1995, Winnipeg in 1995, and Saskatchewan in 1997. His best year with Saskatchewan was 1997, throwing 19 touchdowns, eight interceptions, and completing 62 percent of his passes for 3,721 yards. But he was again cut in the summer of 2000.

In **1990, Major Harris of West Virginia** was the 12th round, 317th pick of Oakland. He never threw a pass in the NFL. He decided to go to Canada. "If Major Harris were playing now, he could play quarterback because he didn't just beat you with his legs, he beat you with his arm." says Ja'Juan Seider, former quarterback who also played at West Virginia.

Clemente Gordon of Grambling was the 11th round, 296th pick of Cleveland in 1990. He was later cut and signed by Dallas, but never threw a pass. Gordon eventually ended up in Canada.

Alabama State's Ricky Jones was the eighth round, 198th pick of the St. Louis Rams in 1992, but he never played in the NFL.

Notre Dame's Tony Rice took over as the starter in the fourth game of his sophomore year because of an injury to Terry Andrysiak. In 1988, he led the Fighting Irish to a 12-0 record and a 31-30 upset over top-ranked Miami in October. The same year, the Irish won their 11th national title. In 1989, he led the team to a 12-1 record and number two ranking. He was not drafted to the NFL. Rice spent one year with Saskatchewan in the Canadian Football League and two years with the Barcelona Dragons of the World League.

Nebraska's Tommy Frazier led the Cornhuskers to back-to-back national championships with his strong running and passing skills. Frazier was MVP in both games, and at one point was Nebraska's all-time leader in total offense (5436), rushing touchdowns for a quarterback (36), and passing touchdowns (43). He also won the Johnny Unitas award for being the best college quarterback. But in 1996, the NFL scouts ignored his accomplishments because he was what they considered an "option quarterback." They considered him a run first, throw last kind of player. In his case, he wasn't drafted at all. Seven rounds of the draft, and nobody wanted him. He ended up playing a few years in the Canadian league. Meanwhile, quarterbacks like Kyle Wacholtz of USC (seventh round pick by Green Bay), Jon Stark of Trinity (seventh round pick by Baltimore), Spence Fischer of Duke (sixth round pick by Pittsburgh), and Michael Crawley of James Madison (sixth round pick by Indianapolis) were all drafted.

Approaching the late '70s and early '80s, there still wasn't much change. **Walter Lewis (Alabama)** was the first Black quarterback at Alabama under coach Bear Bryant. He was first team all-conference in 1983. Lewis was drafted in 1984 by New England in the 3rd round (70th pick) of the 84 supplemental drafts. The supplemental draft was created to keep college players from the new league USFL. Lewis never played in the NFL, but ended up playing in the United States Football League with the Memphis Showboats 1984 and 1985. He finished his career in 1986 in the Canadian league with Montreal.

Also in the 1984 supplemental draft, 5'11" **Turner Gill (Nebraska)** was drafted by the New York Jets in the 3rd round (64th pick). He never played in the NFL. Gill was drafted in major league baseball. He decided to play baseball and eventually played football in Canada. After his playing days, he became the quarterback coach at his alma mater, Nebraska.

While most of Black quarterbacks did come from historically Black schools, Walter Lewis and Turner Gill played at major Division I schools. They played on ranked teams. They played on winning teams. They led their teams to major bowl games. Gill led his team to the national championship even though they lost to Miami. Yet, the opportunity to play quarterback in the NFL just didn't present itself.

Homer Jordan (Clemson 1979-83) led his team to the national championship in 1981 beating Nebraska. He was drafted in 1983 by the United States Football League Washington Federals. He opted to play in Canada. In 1987 he was a backup for Brian Sipes with the Cleveland Browns but did not throw a pass.

In 1951 Bennie Custis (Syracuse) was drafted by the NFL Cleveland Browns. The ban on Black quarterbacks was over, but at this point there had not been a Black quarterback in 30 years. Cleveland wanted Bennie to switch from quarterback to safety. Custis refused and the Browns released him on the condition he wouldn't play for another team.

He signed in the Canadian league with Hamilton. He was the first Black quarterback in Canada and started every game in 1951. He was an all-star quarterback but was moved to running back in 1952. His career ended in 1956 with Ottawa as a running back.

Sandy Stephens (Minnesota 1959-1961) was the first Black quarterback to be named All-American. He was drafted in the second round by Cleveland in the NFL and 5th round by the AFL New York Jets. Both teams wanted him to play another position, so Sandy decided to go to Canada to play for Montreal. Two years after a near fatal car accident in 1964, he signed with Kansas City as a fullback. His career ended in 1968.

Henry Burris (Temple) played most of his career in Canada from 1997-2007 (Calgary Stampeders, Saskatchewan Roughriders). He passed for 37,464 yards and 237 touchdowns. He also ran for 3,922 yards and 51 touchdowns. In 2002 he was a free agent with the Chicago Bears. Burris had 207 yards passing, 3 touchdowns, and 104 rushing yards in a short run with the team.

Casey Printers (Florida A&M) played in Canada from 2003-2010 (British Columbia Lions, Hamilton Tiger Cats). He passed for 11,647 yards, 64 touchdowns. He rushed for 1,467 yards and 19 touchdowns. Printers was CFL's Most Outstanding Player in 2004. During the 2006-2007 NFL season, he signed with the Kansas City Chiefs. He passed for 109 yards, 0 touchdowns in his only season in Kansas.

During the NFL strike of 1987, a few Black players from Canada played as backups for a few weeks.

Bernard Quarles (Washington State) CFL: 1983-1986 (Calgary Stampeders, Ottawa Rough Riders, Saskatchewan Roughriders), 6,529 passing yards and 31 touchdowns.

NFL: 1987 (Los Angeles Rams), 40 passing yards, 1 touchdown, and 8 rushing yards, 0 touchdowns.

Mark Stevens (Utah) CFL: 1985-1986 (Montreal Alouettes), 484 passing yards, and 2 touchdowns. NFL: 1987 (San Francisco 49ers), 52 passing yards, 1 touchdown, and 45 rushing yards, 1 touchdown.

Walter Briggs (Montclair State) signed in 1987 with the New York Jets was 0-2 on passes with 1 interception.

Willie Gillus (Norfolk State) signed in 1987 with Green Bay completed 2-5 passes for 28 yards. Gillus played 5 seasons in Canada.

Tony Robinson (Tennessee 1982-85) had a successful career at the University of Tennessee until he blew out his knee against Alabama his senior year. His season was over early and soon his future would be. He was arrested for cocaine distribution in Knoxville a few weeks after the season ended. He was on probation and playing in Richmond when the 1987 NFL strike happened. He ended up signing with Washington as a replacement backup quarterback. In the third and final replacement game on October 19 against Dallas, he replaced Ed Rupert. In the second quarter, Robinson led Washington to an upset 13-7. He completed 11-18 passes for 152 yards and 2 interceptions. Once the strike ended, Tony was cut, and his NFL career was over.

"When you draft someone in the first round, at some point in time they get an opportunity to either succeed or fail. I don't think I was given a chance."

— Andre Ware

Heisman trophy winner 1989

CHAPTER 5:

INTENTIONAL GROUNDING

B Y THE '90S, NFL OWNERS, MANAGEMENT, AND COACHES continued to ignore the accomplishments of Black quarterbacks in college. No matter how well they threw, ran, or won big games, there was still no guarantee at being drafted. In 1988, University of **Houston sophomore Andre Ware** (6'2", 215 pounds) set a Southwest Conference record with 25 touchdown passes and only eight interceptions. That was just a sign of things to come.

In 1989, Ware exploded onto the college football scene. He had one of the best college football seasons of any quarterback in NCAA history. He set 26 NCAA records. In the first ten games of the 1989 season, the Galveston, Texas native completed 329 passes in 516 attempts for 4,699 yards (NCAA record) and 44 touchdowns. Against arch-rival Texas, Ware had four touchdown passes in leading the Cougars to a 47-9 victory. Against Texas Tech, Ware completed 37 passes for 475 yards and 4 touchdowns.

Andre Ware became the 55th winner of the Heisman Trophy. He was the first Black quarterback to ever win the Heisman Trophy and the first player since Earl Campbell (1977) from the Southwest Conference to earn this honor. With phenomenal statistics as a passer, there was no doubt that he had gotten the attention of NFL scouts. So in the 1990 draft, the Detroit Lions made him the seventh player chosen in the first round. At the time, it was the highest pick a Black quarterback had ever been drafted by an NFL team. While Ware seemed to be on an undeniable path to greatness in the pros, life in Detroit quickly turned into years of sitting on the bench, empty promises, and frustration.

"I was just basically caught in a situation where I played for a head coach that really didn't understand that position very much," Ware explained. "When you say fair, when you draft someone in the first round, at some point in time they get an opportunity to either succeed or fail. I don't thinkI was given [a chance at] either one of them."

It was a rough start from the beginning. Ware missed most of training camp his rookie season because of a contract dispute. When he did join the team, he served as third stringer behind another Black quarterback, Rodney Peete, and Erick Kramer for three straight years.

"Rodney Peete and I were good friends. Coach Wayne Fontes didn't know what to do with us. Rodney and I were always in competition. We wondered how we both got here, and why we were in Detroit. Why would he start one week, and I would start the next."

During his rookie year, he only completed 13 of 30 passes for 164 yards. In 1992, Ware played in four games and completed 50 of 86 passes (58%) for 677 yards, 2 touchdowns, and 4 interceptions.

"At the end of one season, one of the assistant coaches told me to get ready. We only had four games left and we were not going to the playoffs. He said I would finish out the season. But that didn't happen," said Ware.

He wasn't comfortable sitting on the bench. "I wanted to play. After I saw I wasn't going to get a chance to get the starting job, I asked for a trade. They said no. There was actually a deal on the table to trade me to Houston, but they said no. Coach Fontes told me that I would be there for the next ten years."

After four frustrating years with the Lions, Ware was traded to the Minnesota Vikings, who had Warren Moon as their starter. He thought it was a new beginning of his career, but he would never get the opportunity to throw another pass in the NFL.

"In Minnesota, Denny (Coach Dennis Green) felt they were in a position for a playoff run. Having not played a whole lot in Detroit really set me back. They had Sean Salisbury the year before who was a starter. Warren had come in and he was the starter. Of course, Brad Johnson was on that team as well. What happened was, Salisbury signed in Houston and got cut. They offered him the job before they offered it to Warren, so when the opportunity arose to sign him again, that's what Denny chose to do. In case something happened to Warren, he would have a more experienced backup behind Warren."

After being cut by the Vikings, Ware ended up in Jacksonville when the expansion team picked him up, which led to another bad situation that didn't work out.

"They drafted Steve Beuerlein in the expansion draft. Mark Brunell came in from Green Bay, and Rob Johnson was drafted in the fourth round. It just seemed like the wrong place at the wrong time in a couple of different scenarios."

Eventually after being cut by Jacksonville, Ware went North of the border to the Canadian league where many other Black quarterbacks had found success. He joined the Ottawa Rough Riders in 1995, signing as a free agent. Ware completed 70 of 126 passes for 759 yards and three touchdowns with eight interceptions in seven games. He also rushed for 148 yards on 20 carries. Additionally, he played four games with British Columbia before being released when the club acquired veteran Damon Allen. Ware completed 49 of 97 passes for 590 yards and five touchdowns with only two interceptions. He also rushed for 108 yards on 14 carries.

Ware then played for the Toronto Argonauts. It was his third team in three years. Unfortunately, Doug Flutie was Toronto's starting quarterback and led the Argos to the 1996 Grey Cup (Canadian Football Championship).

"That was a lot of fun. I actually enjoyed the game up there. I played quite a bit, and just enjoyed it as a whole."

In 1999, Ware tried to return to the NFL, signing as a free agent with the Oakland Raiders. He was assigned to the developmental league in NFL Europe, but injuries and lack of motivation cut his comeback short and put an end to his football career.

"I tried to come back, but I didn't have the fire burning inside me anymore. So I decided to do something else."

Even though a potential great football career didn't work out, Andre Ware looks at his short career as a benefit for the Black quarterbacks who are in the league today.

"Back then, Blacks were not given the opportunity to play the position. I think if I had come out now, it could have been a different story.

"I have no regrets. I have built a lot of relationships. It has given me an education and it put me in a position for a great life. I am glad for that. I played football to go to college and get a degree. It just so happens that I ended up in the pros."

Ware started his own computer business in Houston, Texas and eventually went into sports broadcasting.

Florida State Quarterback Charlie Ward (1989-1993) was the best player in college football in 1993. He led Florida State to the national championship and won the Heisman trophy. Given pro football's history with black quarterbacks, Ward had another plan besides waiting on the NFL to call him. He went to the NBA to play pro basketball. In addition to being the best quarterback in college football , Ward was the point guard on the Florida State basketball team. The Heisman trophy winner was drafted by the NBA's New York Knicks. He was not drafted at all by any NFL team. Here is another case of a quarterback doing everything possible and still getting ignored by the NFL. In 1993, the Thomasville, Georgia native became the first Seminole player to win the Heisman Trophy award and the second Black quarterback to win the award.

During the 1993 season, Ward was considered to be the nation's premier quarterback. He stood at the height of 6'2". He had the speed and quickness, averaging six yards a carry. He played at a Division One powerhouse program in Florida State. Ward completed 70% of his passes and had six 300-yard passing games. Ward led Florida State to the national championship, but the NFL scouts were not impressed. Ward was never drafted in the NFL.

"I was supposed to be the best, the Heisman winner. It didn't make sense that I was *not* going to be a top pick."

Ward, who had also been a star basketball player at FSU, was drafted in the first round by the New York Knickerbockers of the NBA.

"I gave the first opportunity to the NFL, and the NFL didn't give me an opportunity," Ward said. "They came up with excuses about why they didn't draft me. That I was not big enough. That I was too short and didn't have a strong enough arm, and everyone was afraid that if they drafted me in the first round, I wouldn't play football," Ward said in a 2000 interview.

However, the Baltimore Colts drafted John Elway in the first round of 1983, in spite of the fact that he said he was going to play pro baseball. One person even said that Ward was not your prototype NFL quarterback! This in spite of the fact he was the best quarterback in the NCAA and other not so talented quarterbacks were drafted. Ward is the only Heisman winner to not get drafted by the NFL. Several other players faced similar problems on the field.

In 1981, **Southern Mississippi's Reggie Collier** was the first quarterback in NCAA history to pass for 1000 yards and throw 1000 yards. Collier finished ninth in Heisman voting as Southern Miss finished ninth in rankings.

He was drafted by the Dallas Cowboys in the sixth round of the 1983 draft. However, he decided to take a more lucrative contract and played in USFL with Birmingham Stallions. He joined Dallas after the league folded. In 1986, he played four games and completed eight of 15 passes (53%) for 96 yards, 1 touchdown, and 2 interceptions. The next year in 1987, Collier signed with the Pittsburgh Steelers and played two games, completing 4 of 7 passes (57%) for 110 yards, 2 touchdowns, and 1 interception. Over his career, he played in six games and completed 12 of 22 passes (54%) for 206 yards, 3 touchdowns, and 3 interceptions. Collier would not get another opportunity to play in the NFL.

In 1986, Washington state quarterback Ricky Turner made a brief appearance with the Baltimore Colts. In 1986, he spent a couple of seasons in the Canadian league before coming to the NFL. The former Washington State player signed as a free agent with the Indianapolis Colts. Turner, who was only six feet tall, played in four games and completed three of four passes (75%) and 16 rushes for 42 yards and 2 touchdowns. That was his only chance in the NFL.

Virginia's Shawn Moore also burst upon the college football scene with a big, strong arm. From 1987-1990, he completed 421 of 762 passes (55%) for 6,629 yards, and threw 55 touchdowns and 32 interceptions. He also rushed for 1,268 yards and 28 touchdowns. He set a school record, tossing 21 touchdowns in one season. His 6,629 career passing yards and 421 completions are all Virginia records. In 1991, the Denver

Broncos picked Virginia's all-time leading passer in the 11th round with the 284th pick. After sitting on the bench at the start of his career, Moore played in an alternate possession system with backup Jeff Lewis after John Elway got hurt in 1992. Moore, who stood 6'2" and 210 pounds, never got a chance to earn the starting job full-time. He played every other possession in three games in 1992 and completed 17 of 34 passes (50%) for 232 yards, 3 interceptions, and 39 yards rushing. The Martinsville, Virginia native was eventually traded to Arizona and cut by the start of the season. Moore never got another chance. He ended up playing a few years in the Canadian league with Ottawa and Winnipeg.

At this point, a Black quarterback getting drafted in the NFL was not uncommon, but making the team and actually getting to play was a different story. Here are some of those quarterbacks.

In 1975, University of Tampa **quarterback Freddie Solomon** was picked by the Miami Dolphins. He was immediately converted to wide receiver. By 1978, he was playing with the San Francisco 49ers. That year as an emergency quarterback, he completed 5 of 10 passes for 85 yards.

Brian Mitchell (quarterback turned NFL running back 1990-2003) was a successful quarterback at Southwestern Louisiana who ran the options to perfection. "I had no issues in college. I was welcomed because my coach at the time, Nelson Stokely, believed in playing the best. I was the only Black QB while I was there, and I quickly became the starter."

When it was time to go pro, Washington selected Mitchell as a running back and kick returner in the fifth round of the 1990 draft.

"It was a combination. The league wasn't looking at me as a QB. They drafted me as an athlete. I could have gone to Canada and played QB, but my dream was to play in the NFL, not Canada. I didn't care what position because I felt I had the ability to do other things."

Mitchell turned into one of the greatest return specialists in NFL history. He is in Washington's Ring of Fame with other Washington football legends. He finished his career with 14,014 kickoffs return yards and 4,999 punt return yards.

Damon Allen (Cal State Fullerton) played in the Canadian league from 1985-2008 for numerous teams. Allen won the championship Grey Cup in 1987 (MVP), 1993 (MVP), 2000, 2004 (MVP). At age 42, he was CFL's Most Outstanding Player. He retired with 72,381 yards passing, which was the most ever for a Canadian player.

"*...the ignorant folks that call it Black quarterback, as opposed to looking at it as a quarterback with a lot of talent.*"

– *Kordell Stewart*
quarterback 1995-2005

CHAPTER 6:

SACKED

THE ATTITUDES BY COACHES AND OWNERS ABOUT BLACK quarterbacks continued to be an issue well into the '90s. Teams looked for and drafted mostly the classic drop back, immobile quarterbacks who would sit in the pocket and pass. The league had added more teams and a few more Black players were getting chances, yet still the number of starting Black quarterbacks and backups on NFL rosters was small.

"I hate to sit here and talk about Black quarterbacks–a guy who is at the position is a quarterback. But I think it's the ignorant folks that call it 'Black quarterback,' as opposed to looking at it as a quarterback with a lot of talent. He is getting away from the traditional mold," said **Pittsburgh quarterback Kordell Stewart.**

"That's the most irritating part of it for me. People look at it as a Black quarterback. It had to be Black and White issues when it was actually an issue of a guy going out and doing his job and wanting to just play the game he loves to play. It just so happens that you have guys of all types of nationalities playing in the league. Running backs that are Black, running backs that are White. But it seems you have to go to this position and call it a Black and White issue. That's the most irritating thing of it all. The best thing that we can do—not just as Black quarterbacks, but as people—is to look at it as an opportunity, change, and not get caught up in the racial side of it all."

Stewart of Colorado was the second round, 60th pick of the Pittsburgh Steelers. In college, the second team All-American set school all-time records with 456 completions and 7,770 yards in total offense. He initially made his mark in the NFL as a multi-talented player who played not just quarterback but also wide receiver and running back.

"It's almost like playing a game of chess. You can never let them know what you're thinking. It's just a matter of just going out there and playing and performing, just doing what I can do best, let everything else take care of itself. Control what you can. The rest don't worry about it," Stewart says.

Stewart had a number of up and down seasons that included some playoff games, being benched, regaining his starting job, and being benched again. His most consistent season as a passer was 2001. He completed 266 of 442 (60%) passes for 3,109 yards with 14 touchdown passes and 11 interceptions. He also rushed for 534 yards and 5 touchdowns.

Stewart led the 13-3 Steelers to the division title and into the playoffs, and they were expected to get to the Super Bowl. However, the team lost to the eventual Super Bowl champion New England Patriots. It was the second time the team had come within a game of the Super Bowl. Eventually he lost his job to Tommy Maddox and left for Chicago. Stewart never found any kind of success. He played his final game in Baltimore as an emergency player before being cut.

Three years before Steve McNair and Kordell Stewart came into the NFL, **Jeff Blake** started his NFL career as an emergency quarterback. From the beginning, it was a struggle for Blake to even get on the field. As he was preparing for college, he declined a scholarship to UCLA because they wanted to move him to defensive back. He opted to go to East Carolina. It turned out to be a good choice. As a senior, he led the Pirates to an 11-1 record and the school's highest ranking in the polls (9th). He finished in the Top Ten in the Heisman Trophy voting and was an honorable mention All-American.

In 1992, Blake was the 166th pick in the sixth round by the Jets. In his rookie season, Blake played in three games and completed four of nine passes. That was it. The Jets cut him at the end of the year. The next year Blake signed with Cincinnati as an emergency third quarterback. He did not play in any regular season game. 1994 was his breakout year, thanks to injuries to the other two quarterbacks. He was AFC Offensive Player of the Month for November and completed eight passes of 50-plus yards. His ability to throw the deep ball and his accuracy allowed him to keep the job. The next year as a starter, Blake tossed 28 touchdown passes and 17 interceptions. But winning and making the payoffs was still not happening. The year 1996 was another great one for Blake. During this season his 308 completions were the second most in club history behind his own mark of 326 set in the previous year. He threw for 3,624 passing yards, which was the fourth best in team history at the time. He finished that year with 24 touchdown passes and only 14 interceptions.

Blake's success did not mean success for the Bengals. Cincinnati still could not make the playoffs. For the next couple of seasons, the Bengals ownership failed to upgrade the talent on the team. The coaches were hired and fired. The only consistency was losing.

Eventually the lack of a supporting cast took its toll on Jeff Blake. He was injured the next season and then lost his job to free agent Neil O'Donnell the year after that. By 1999, Blake had regained his starting position. The Bengals had drafted Oregon's Akili Smith to be the quarterback of the future.

After the first week against Tennessee, Blake was injured again. Rookie Akili Smith took over but the team continued to lose. In Week 4 after the Bengals went 0-4, Blake would reclaim the job. His performance included more than 300 yards passing and three touchdowns in Week 11, passed for 241 yards, one rushing touchdown, and one passing touchdown in the Week 12 win over the Steelers. In Week 13, Blake completed 21 of 30 passes for 334 yards and four touchdowns against the 49ers. Still, winning was not in the cards. They finished the season 4-12, and his roller coaster ride in Ohio was over.

In February 2000, Blake signed as a free agent with the New Orleans Saints. It was a four-year contract worth $17 million to be the starter. The Saints were a team similar to Cincinnati in the fact that they'd had very little success in the past. After a slow start, things turned and started to turn for this franchise. Blake led the team down the field for the game-winning drive, completing an eight-yard touchdown to Joe Horne for a 28-27 win over San Diego. He completed 33 of 47 passes for 259 yards and 3 touchdowns.

The Saints would drop the next two games before beating Chicago 31-10. He rushed for 65 yards, completed 18 of 25 passes for 232 yards and 3 touchdowns. They would go on to beat Carolina, Atlanta, San Francisco, and Carolina again for their fifth win in a row. All of a sudden, this struggling franchise was on their way to the playoffs. As luck would have it, in the next game against the Raiders, Blake broke his foot, and the season was over. That injury was the end of the road for Blake in New Orleans. It allowed **Aaron Brooks** to take the field and continue the Saints' playoff run and eventual playoff win.

By the time Blake came back from his injury in the 2001 season, he could not get his job from Brooks. He would only throw one pass that season. He was released in February 2002. From this point on, Blake became a journeyman quarterback. He signed a one-year contract as a backup with the Baltimore

Ravens. During the 2002 season, Blake started the last 10 games of the season. Eventually he signed a three-year contract with the Arizona Cardinals to be the starter. He only played one year with the bad Cardinals before booking to Philly as a backup and finishing his playing days with a short stay in Chicago.

As the mid 1990s saw the emergence of Jeff Blake, other quarterbacks began to at least get a chance to make it in the NFL. In addition to Steve McNair in Houston and Kordell Stewart in Pittsburgh, **Michigan State's Tony Banks was drafted.** He was a 1996 second round, 42nd pick of the St. Louis Rams, and the first quarterback taken in the draft that year.

Banks' rookie year with the struggling franchise would be a struggle once he became the starter. The Rams were a dismal team that finished last in their division. It's where the Rams would stay during his time as the starter. By the end of the 1998 season, Banks was done with the Rams. On April 17, 1999, he was traded to Baltimore.

In his first year with the Baltimore Ravens, Banks was demoted to third string by new coach Brian Billick because he wouldn't tuck in his jersey. He sat behind Scott Mitchell and Stoney Case. When high-priced Scott Mitchell failed miserably as the starter, the team turned to newly acquired Stoney Case. The results did not change. In an act of desperation, Banks was named the starter by Game 6. The Ravens had started the season 2-4, but with Banks as the starter, they went 6-4. He passed for 274 yards in Week 11 victory, and in Week 13, he led the Ravens to a 41-14 win over the Tennessee Titans. He completed 18 of 31 passes for 332 yards and four touchdown passes (76 yards, 6 yards, one yard, and 39 yards). Banks threw three touchdowns and over 200 yards in a Week 14 win over Pittsburgh. The Ravens improved to 6-7. The next game, Week 15, Banks completed 24 of 36 passes for 298 yards, three interceptions, and three touchdowns (34-yard, six-yard, 47-yard) as Baltimore won 31-8 over New Orleans. The Ravens improved to 7-7. In Week 16, Ravens improved to 8-7 with a 22-0 win over Cincinnati. Banks completed 15-33 for 187 yards, 1 touchdown, and 1 interception. In the regular season finale, Banks completed 18 of 26 passes for 163 yards, no touchdowns, and one interception as the Ravens' streak ended with a loss to New England 20-3. In the 12 games he played in, Banks threw for 2,136 yards, 17 touchdowns, and 8 interceptions.

In 2000, the expectations were high for Baltimore. They had finished the previous year with a stiff defense and a young, strong-armed quarterback leading the offense. On opening day, Banks completed 18 of 32 passes for 199 yards and one touchdown in a victory over Pittsburgh. The following week, he threw a career-high five touchdowns, including the game winner with 41 seconds remaining to Shannon Sharpe to beat Jacksonville 39-36. In addition to the touchdown passes, Banks completed 23 of 40 passes for 262 yards in a 17-point come-from-behind win.

The team won three of the next four games, but the offense was less than spectacular.

For two consecutive weeks, Baltimore failed to score a touchdown. The Ravens lost the next game 10-3 to Washington. It was the third week in a row Baltimore failed to score a touchdown. Banks completed a modest 16 of 27 passes for 135 yards and one interception. The pressure was beginning to mount for the team and the quarterback, in spite of their 5-1 record. The next week, they lost again to the Tennessee Titans 14-6. Banks completed 17 of 32 passes for 229 yards. Unfortunately, he threw three interceptions, including one in the end zone that killed a scoring drive. He threw another one to linebacker Randall Godfrey that was returned for a touchdown. It was the beginning of the end for Banks. He was benched in the second half of that game and replaced by Trent Dilfer. Still, Baltimore lost. The Ravens were 5-2 when Coach Brian Billick benched Banks and decided Trent Dilfer would start the rest of the year.

The following week, with Trent Dilfer starting, Baltimore was beaten by Pittsburgh and still did not score a touchdown. In fact, Dilfer fumbled in the red zone in the first drive that the Steelers recovered. Dilfer finished with a modest number, completing 11 of 24 passes for 152 yards, no touchdowns, and one interception, yet he remained the starter. The Ravens eventually started to win games with their strong defense, but the offense remained ineffective. It was the Baltimore defense and special teams that carried them all the way through the playoffs and to Super Bowl victory. Banks played on one possession in the Super Bowl and threw one incomplete pass. It was his last pass with Baltimore. He finished the season completing 150 of 274 passes for 1,578 yards, 8 touchdowns, and 8 interceptions.

After he was cut by Baltimore in March of 2001, Banks signed with Dallas, but to his surprise, he was cut before pre-season even started when the Dallas coaches decided to go with rookie **Quincy Carter**. Banks eventually signed as a free agent backup with Washington. After a miserable 0-5 start where the team did not score a touchdown with Jeff George running the show, Banks took over. Jeff George was cut. The team rebounded to finish 8-8. But at the end of the year, the team still didn't make the playoffs. The coach was fired, the Skins went looking for a new quarterback, and Banks was once again on the free agent market. Banks completed 198 of 370 passes (53%) for 2,386 yards, 10 touchdowns, and 10 interceptions. He also rushed for 2 touchdowns and 152 yards.

During a workout in the off season, Banks injured his hand. The injury required surgery and kept him from signing with a new team. In 2002, he signed on as a backup quarterback with the expansion Houston Texans. He started a game here and there due to injuries, but Banks never got another chance to succeed like he had done in Baltimore and Washington.

In the same year Tony Banks entered the NFL, **Rutgers' Ray Lucas signed as a free agent with the New England**

Patriots. In college, Lucas had set Rutgers records with 43 career touchdowns, 514 completions, and 908 attempts. He was not drafted and in 1996 he signed as a free agent receiver with the New England Patriots to play on special teams. The next year he was cut, and the New York Jets picked him up as a receiver. After being waived, Lucas ran the scout team offenses and played receiver. In November, he was added to the 53-man roster as a backup QB to Neil O'Donnell. In Game 12 against Minnesota, Lucas ran once for 15 yards. In the season finale against Detroit, Lucas not only ran for 30 yards, he completed three of four passes for 28 yards. It was his only action as a quarterback that year. Through injuries and a lack of production, Lucas got his shot to be a full-time starter the next year. The Jets had a 6-2 record under his leadership. The next year the Jets drafted Marshall University quarterback Chad Pennington. He was the first quarterback taken in the draft.

It was also a free agent year for Lucas who did not get the big contract he hoped for after his 1999 performance. On March 16, 2001, Lucas officially signed as a free agent with the Miami Dolphins to back up Jay Feidler. In 2002, Lucas replaced and injured Jay Feidler when the Dolphins were 4-2. With Lucas at the helm, the Dolphins went 2-4. He did not play well at all during that stretch. Miami did not make the playoffs. In the off season, a few days after the NFL draft, Lucas was released. The next year he was signed as an emergency third string quarterback with Baltimore, but he never played again in the NFL.

Two years after Tony Banks and Ray Lucas came into the NFL, **Charlie Batch of Eastern Michigan was the second round, 60th pick of the Detroit Lions.** In 1998, the rookie got his first start September 16 replacing Scott Mitchell. He played in the last 12 games. His season ended early after he had a fracture in his lower back against San Francisco. Batch ended his first year throwing 136 straight pass attempts without an interception (six games). That tied him with Cleveland's Bernie Kosar (1985) for the longest streak in NFL history by a rookie. His passer rating of 83.3 is the fourth-best mark ever by a rookie.

The following year, Batch led Detroit to a 6-2 start without Barry Sanders (who suddenly retired just before the season). In the first half of Week 9, Batch suffered a broken right thumb. Nonetheless, he returned in Week 16 and replaced an ineffective Gus Frerotte.

The rest of Batch's time with the Lions was filled with injuries, inconsistencies, and defeat. In the 2000 season, again it was injuries that slowed down Batch's development. He broke a bone near his knee in mini-camp so he did not start opening day because of the injury. By 2002, Detroit had released him. In June 2002, he signed with the Steelers as a backup. Eventually, the Steelers drafted Ben Rothlisberger. Batch tore up his knee and big Rothlisberger became the backup to Tommy Maddox. Rothlisberger replaced him and would eventually guide the team to a Super Bowl win over Seattle. Batch remained the backup.

During the '90s, although the quarterbacks were getting drafted, the chance to play or be developed into a starter or backup were still slim.

In 1994, Howard University's star quarterback Jay Walker was the seventh round, 198th pick of New England. While he did make the team, he did not throw a pass as a rookie. Walker was eventually assigned by Patriots to Barcelona Dragons in 1995 World League developmental league in 1995. By August he was released. He signed with the Minnesota Vikings on March 15, 1996. Walker got his only NFL game experience in a December game. He completed two of two passes for 31 yards. He remained with Minnesota in 1997 but he was cut by the start of the 1998 season. Eventually Walker ended up as a backup quarterback in the Canadian Football League and never got back to the NFL. Years later he went into broadcasting and later became a Maryland state delegate.

In 1996, Wally Richardson of Penn State was the seventh round, 234th pick of Baltimore. Richardson was a four-time all-academic conference player. The 6'4" passer was a third string emergency player in 1997. He did not play in any games. The next year, Baltimore sent Wally to the NFL in Europe to play for the England Monarchs. Richardson made his first and only appearance in an NFL game in December 1998. Wally completed one of two passes for one yard. The next year in 1999, Baltimore cut Wally. In December, he signed with Atlanta as third quarterback after Chris Chandler and Danny Kannell both got hurt. He went into the 2000 training camp with the Atlanta Falcons but was cut and out of the league before the start of the season.

Dameyune Craig (6'1", 200 pounds) of Auburn in 1997 signed as a free agent with Carolina as an emergency quarterback. When Dameyune Craig was a high school freshman in Alabama, the coaches moved him to quarterback because of his arm strength. The junior varsity team ended up winning the last games of the season. "They moved me up to varsity the last game.I love to win so I want to play quarterback because he touches the ball every play. This guy determines whether or not you win a game."

At that point, Craig was determined to be an NFL quarterback. The problem was when he looked at the pro game, there were not that many Black quarterbacks playing. He knew the deck was stacked against him from the start. At the time it was Warren Moon, Doug Williams, Randall Cunningham, and Vince Evans playing for the Raiders. They were all bigger than Craig. He saw his size as another card in the deck that was already stacked against him. He says he knew he had to not only win, but perform at a high level and study the history of Black quarterbacks in college and the pros.

"We go on to the state championships. I was at a school that never won anything, not even a playoff game. They moved me to quarterback; we won the state championship my sophomore year. I broke my arm my junior year. We won again my senior year."

Craig was in the record books; he was a winner. Now he had to navigate being recruited to top level football programs and avoid being switched to another position or not being coached to play in the pros. "I came from a poor neighborhood near my high school. My coach was Ben Harris. Ben Harris played at Alabama State, he was 65 and he threw the ball. My favorite quarterback coming up was Dan Marino. Coach Ben had a release like Dan Marino and a stronger one. He actually told me, 'you're going to be a good quarterback.' He made me a good quarterback and developed me and wanted to see that happen. He would teach me about all these guys. I started learning about Black quarterbacks first, and Black college quarterbacks, and that's why I know all these people. So I'm coming out of high school and I was willing to look at Black colleges because I knew I had to make it out of here. Black colleges didn't even start looking at me until the season was over. I even took a visit to Jackson State. Alcorn State came in and said, 'You can sit for a year; we got a quarterback [Steve McNair] who is going early to the NFL.' I was like, 'Who is he?' 'Steve McNair. You can play behind him for a year.' I'm not sitting behind anybody. I looked up and Air McNair was killing it. I was like, 'This man really is good.'

"When you talk about Don McPherson and Shawn Moore, they ran the option but they could throw the ball too, but I didn't want to go to that type of offense. When I made my decision to go to college, I wasn't going to any school with an option; that was my number one rule because what I know once I pitch, I knew I was going to be viewed as an athlete.

"So coming out I'm looking at Charlie Ward. Charlie Ward looked like me throwing the ball. He spreads out, he's killing it, so I patterned my game after Charlie Ward. I wanted to go to a school that teaches me like that. I knew when I went to school I had to go above and beyond others. That's why I knew I had to win state championships in high school. So I put that pressure on myself so I could handle that," Craig says. "I said I'm going to have to go to the school where I'm throwing the ball. Not only throw on the bar but I might have to break every record at the school. Just to even get looked at. Back then it was different. My mind was different from everybody else's. I want to stay at that position. It wasn't that I'm just an athlete. So when I get there I can move. In my mind I said, 'I'm a quarterback. I've had success. So in order to stay here, this is what I'm going to have to do.' So I was setting myself up for that."

Craig also wanted to go to a school that had already played Black quarterbacks. He was being recruited by all the top programs. Mississippi State had two Black quarterbacks—Sleepy Robinson and Greg Plummer. West Virginia had Major Harris, who was a Heisman candidate. Tony Rice was quarterback at Notre Dame. Craig looked at schools that had successful starting Black quarterbacks and a pro-style offense that showcased his arm. "I want to look at a pro staff system that throws the ball. Any school that I went to, I was going to have to be the only quarterback brought in that year. Not because I was afraid of competition but because I wanted reps. I wanted to show the coaches that I could play the position. Nobody is giving me advice; I'm doing this on my own, I'm planning my life out."

At the time, Alabama had just won the national championship. Auburn had a coaching change. Craig had committed to University of Southern Mississippi after the recruiters promised him that he would be the only quarterback in that class, but then he says the school went back on their word and recruited another quarterback. Heath Graham. Graham ended up taking Craig's spot. "They told me, 'Well, we took him because he was a local kid.' I said, 'Well, y'all lied to me, and if you lie to me now, you will lie to me later.'"

Craig ended up not going to Southern Mississippi. Mississippi State was next on the list. NFL coordinator Bruce Arians had joined the staff with head coach Jackie Sherill to run a pro style system.

"He had just come from the pros. I was probably going to go to Mississippi State. So Jimbo Fisher (assistant coach, Auburn) comes in and says, 'By the time you are a senior we're going to run in the same offense that Florida State was running with Charlie Ward [Florida State Heisman trophy winner].' Auburn coach Terry Bowden was [Florida State coach] Bobby Bowden's son. I looked in their eyes, man, and I saw something in both of their eyes, and I trusted my instincts. I committed to Auburn. By my senior year I'm in the spread system.

"Auburn has started two Black quarterbacks. I was the third Black quarterback. When I was looking at schools, I only looked at schools where they played Black quarterbacks. So that kind of put me in the right direction. You had Pat Washington and Reggie Slack. They both played in the '80s.

"Coach Jimbo Fisher told me during our first scrimmage to run play action. I kept the ball and I ran a 65-yard touchdown and he asked me, 'Why didn't you throw the ball in the flat?' I said, 'Coach, I just thought I could get more yards running it.' But he said, 'Dame, you got a beating with your head first.' I'll never forget that. He said, 'Do you want to be a quarterback or do you want to be done with your arm first and then let your athletic ability take over?' I had a great mentor and coach in Jimbo Fisher. If you look at his record, he's had a lot of quarterbacks in the NFL. There were four Black quarterbacks drafted overall, and at the time he coached Jameis Winston (Florida State) and JaMarcus Russell (LSU). He coached both of those guys."

At Auburn, the Pritchard, Alabama native was a second-team All-SouthEastern Conference selection as a senior. Craig was a Heisman Trophy contender who set an Auburn single-season passing record with 3,277 yards. He was the only quarterback in Auburn history to throw for 3,000 yards.

"They had two Heisman Trophy winners, Pat Sullivan and Cam Newton, and neither one of them threw for 3,000 yards. So I go to the senior bowl and I win the MVP. They wanted to bring in three quarterbacks, but I told them they could only bring in two. If you bring three, I'm not coming. Because I need reps, I need to show him what I'm going to do, and it was in my hometown so I called the shots." Craig recalls.

"That's when things started changing around '99, 2000. I came out too early. The game is changing because they spread the game out these days. The lineman gets so athletic that you can't just be a statue back there, you have to have mobility. I never looked at myself as a running quarterback. I looked at myself as a guy who gets better with my feet. I don't run for a lot of yards at Auburn. Did you look at my rushing stats? I had 300 yards in my career, so what I would do is just buy time. I used the time to scan the field. I knew once people were threatened by that, they would change their rush and try to keep me in the pocket."

NFL draft day came and went, but Craig's name wasn't called. "I was predicted to go mid to late. So I will go to Carolina for my first year. I'm on the practice squad and I'm doing everything but playing quarterback. Kick off team return I'm doing all that stuff on the practice squad."

As a rookie free agent with the Panthers in 1998, Craig spent the first 13 games on the practice team before being signed to the active roster. He never played that year. The next summer, Carolina sent Craig to NFL Europe to play with the Scottish Claymores.

"Before I get there, I'll look at all the records. I'll look at the passing record, the touchdown record in a single game yardage record. I said to myself, 'I gotta break all these records. I gotta break every record in this book.'"

His biggest game was against the Frankfurt Galaxy. He threw for a league record 611 yards and completed 27 of 37 passes for 5 touchdowns with no interceptions. He led the league in just about every passing category.

"The single-game passing record was 500 yards and the single-game touchdown record in the 23 the single-season passing record was 2963 yards. We only played 10 games. You had Kurt Warner play over there. You had John Kitna play over there. You had Jake Delhomme. You also had Danny Wuerfel." Craig said."I'll never forget this. I even threw the 600 yards, I was 27 and 37 five touchdowns six on 11 yards only 237 passes. After the game was over, I said, 'You just broke the record.' So I went home that night, you know what I did? I was depressed. I wasn't happy. I was like, 'How did I throw for 600 yards and five touchdowns and we won the game 38-35?' And you know what I did from that point on? I had six interceptions in the first. I had four interceptions in the first six games".

"At the end of the year I broke the single-game passing record 611 yards in one game, threw for 2,938 yards, and I was 20 or a bit behind record. I was two touchdowns away from breaking the touchdown passes. Theoretically I had the best TV season in history. I come back as the fifth string quarterback. I asked Carolina to trade me. They wouldn't trade me, but they did give me a signing bonus [$80,000] because I was undrafted. The first year I got $30,000."

Craig rejoined Carolina in 1999 but was inactive for all games. The next year he was again an emergency third string quarterback behind Steve Beuerlein and Jeff Lewis. He made his first regular season appearance as a running back. He rushed two times for a loss of one yard.

He appeared again as a running back in Week 12 against Green Bay in a Monday night game. Craig rushed one time for five yards. He finished the 2000 season with no passes and two runs for four yards.

"Ditka was trying to get me to go to the Saints. So Ditka came out to see it but what am I going to trade for him? He had just traded the whole draft for Heisman Trophy winner Ricky Williams. So three years later, ironically Jake Delhomme is taking Carolina to the Super Bowl, and I'm sitting at home. And Jake Delhomme whispering time in NFL Europe with Pat Barnes. The team that I threw for 600 yards against was Jake Delhomme's team."

In 2001, Dameyune Craig sat inactive for all the games until Week 8. He replaced Chris Weinke late in the game and completed his first NFL pass. He completed four of eight passes for 32 yards' passing. He also had 20 rushing yards. Unfortunately, his opportunity was short-lived. With six minutes left in the game, Craig injured his hip. Carolina lost to Miami 23-6 and lost Craig for the year. It was a bad break for Craig, who was a free agent at the end of the year. "Chris Weinke gets hurt, I go into the game. I played three series and ended up tearing two limit ligaments in my foot and basically ended up ending my career. I completed my last four passes, the game slowed down, and I really believe if I would not have gotten hurt, I would've had a long career and could've started in the NFL."

On March 7, 2002, he signed a one-year contract with Washington. He hoped to compete for the quarterback job but was released April 30, 2002. Washington drafted Patrick Ramsey (Tulane), and signed free agent Shane Matthews (Chicago) to join Danny Wuerfull and Sage Rosenfeld.

"That took a toll on my body. I'm in pain now because I was getting hit a lot. So I think I was lucky that I made a lot of good decisions to be around the right people and to get to the right development and get the most out of me. My time at school I wouldn't trade it for the world. I know I was in the deep South at Auburn Alabama, but I was treated well there. I had a great experience in college. Currently I am in College Station.

"I coached in the NFL for a year, and I was working with the scouting department and the way they evaluate. If I hadn't gone through all this stuff probably my mindset would be different. I'm a football coach now. And I have a chart and I say height, weight, speed, and then I go through the intangibles right.

"When you look deep down inside, I think the guys that you look at having success, regardless of the color, they all have the same traits. If you break it down, that's when you get into problems with why you think, when you say why is this guy playing and this guy is not. Well now they say, 'This guy is 6'4" but he still gets a chance and he walks in a room and he looks good. He can throw the ball a long way; he may not be accurate but he looks the part. The guy is a winner.' I think they have certain traits about them that keep them on the field and keep them in a position, I think that position is very unique.

"I had a vision for what I had to do. I don't have a pro typical height or weight so I stayed at the NFL game. I had to do what I had to do to win championships and he would just get enough to win."

"Steve McNair will never be judged fairly when compared to other quarterbacks. People can pretend it's not the case, but there is never a level playing field. The Steve McNair saga proves that."

— Brad Hopkins
Titan teammate

CHAPTER 7:

ALL OUT BLITZ

I WILL NEVER FORGET BEING ASSIGNED TO COVER COLLEGE FOOTBALL in Mississippi during my last year of college. As a beginner in the news business, I had to work the camera, shoot the video, write and edit the story. My first real sports assignment at WAPT (Jackson, Mississippi) was given to me by sports director Mike Rowe. Being a relative rookie in the business, I was assigned to drive 60 miles away to cover Alcorn State football. They just happened to have an up-and-coming player named Steve McNair playing quarterback. From watching this guy play day one, even I knew he was special. At 6'2", he was a massive, strong guy with a quiet personality. But on that field he was running, scrambling, slicing up defenses, and putting Alcorn in the national spotlight. He was the offense. Strong arm, fast, bringing his team from behind week after week. After each game, I would talk to him about his remarkable performance and how he did what he did. Never a man of many words, the soft-spoken on-the-rise-superstar would simply talk about these superhuman plays with a casual, "Aw shucks, I'm just doing my thing" remark. As the legend of "AIR MCNAIR" grew, the national sports media started paying attention. So did the NFL scouts who had started to come to campus. Even film director Spike Lee had to witness "AIR MCNAIR" in person by flying to campus to stand on the sideline for the game against Grambling. And as usual, McNair put on a show, bringing his team from behind with an air assault and ground attack that simply defied logic. Accurate with the long and short pass, running, throwing, and standing in the pocket throwing, spinning away from defenders sometimes to run sometimes to throw. He graced the cover of *Sports Illustrated* his senior year and he was a Heisman trophy finalist. But the *Sports Illustrated* article didn't just highlight the spectacular; it brought up concerns about whether he had a future in the NFL given the history of Black quarterbacks who had come before him. He was big in stature and even bigger in the games. But people were wondering based on the past if he was big enough to overcome the history of the Black quarterback.

McNair was the runner up for the Heisman trophy; he blew people away at the NFL combine. He was drafted by the Houston Oilers (Tennessee Titans).

He spent the first two years on the bench as the team prepared to leave Houston, Texas and move to Nashville, Tennessee.

After playing a season in Memphis while the stadium was being built, McNair became the full-time starter.

In 1995, McNair was the first round, third pick of the Houston Oilers. He was the first Black quarterback ever drafted within the first three picks (highest ever at the time).

In the 1999 off season, the Tennessee Titans signed a much-traveled Neil O'Donnell strictly as a backup to Steve McNair. After one preseason game, McNair went out because of an injury and O'Donnell got the call. It seemed from that point on, some Tennessee fans immediately decided that O'Donnell was the better quarterback. Night in and night out, people were calling talk radio shows saying that McNair was awful and O'Donnell should be the starter.

"How much longer are we going to stick with this McNair guy? He has had five years and he hasn't done a thing," said one caller.

"McNair can't throw. Get rid of him. He is not an NFL quarterback," said the next caller.

The calls kept coming in about how McNair couldn't do this and couldn't do that. At the same time, Neil O'Donnell was being hailed as the answer to any perceived problem. This is the same Neil O'Donnell that threw two interceptions directly into the hands of Dallas cornerback Larry Brown, which cost the Steelers the Super Bowl. After that game, Pittsburgh said farewell to him and let him go into free agency. This was the same Neil O'Donnell that played two seasons with the Jets and was benched in favor of Glenn Foley...yes, Glenn Foley. The next year, Coach Bill Parcells took over the Jets and cut O'Donnell before the season started. This is the same Neil O'Donnell that was brought into Cincinnati to replace Jeff Blake. By the end of the year, the Bengals were still suffering from yet another losing season, and O'Donnell was benched. In the off season, the Bengals released him. He signed with the Titans just a few days before the exhibition season. If he is as great as some Titans fans would have you believe, where are all the playoff wins, passing records, and other teams clamoring or beating down his door to sign him?

In Week 1 of the 1999 NFL season, Steve McNair had a career day against the Cincinnati Bengals (21 of 32 passes for 341 yards and 3 touchdowns). The Titans jumped out to a 21-0 lead behind two McNair touchdown passes, but in the second quarter, the team started to self-destruct. Running back Eddie George fumbled. That led to a Bengals score of 21-7. After a long McNair pass, receiver Yancey Thigpen lost a fumble that led to a Cincinnati score of 21-14 at the half.

A McNair interception in the third quarter led to a Cincinnati field goal. When McNair was sacked and he fumbled, he was showered with boos from some fans. Why wasn't running back Eddie George booed when he fumbled? Why wasn't receiver Yancey Thigpen booed when he fumbled? McNair eventually led the Titans to the game-winning score with a touchdown pass to Eddie George. The next week, Steve McNair was on the injured list and had to have back surgery that put him out for the next six weeks. Some people blamed the Titans conservative offense on McNair.

Now that his backup, Neil O'Donnell, got the job for six weeks, it was going to be better. The Titans kept winning, beating Baltimore, Cleveland, Jacksonville (thanks to a bad Brunell pass from the one-yard line that was intercepted), New Orleans, and a loss to San Francisco to go 5-1. But the offense was still conservative and barely getting by. The following week, the unbeaten 6-0 St. Louis Rams came to Nashville. Steve McNair was set to make his comeback against the best team in the league. McNair threw for two touchdowns and ran for another. Just like in Week 1, the Titans were off to a 21-0 lead. They barely won 24-21. So now, the very fans that had booed him were seemingly on his side again.

Not so fast. The next week against the 5-1 Miami Dolphins, the Titans lost 17-0 behind a constant blitz from one of the best defenses in the league. McNair threw three interceptions to Sam Madison on the exact same route. Titans Coach Jeff Fisher did not bench McNair. Back on Titans radio, the fans' hatred for McNair was resurrected.

"Why didn't he put Neil O'Donnell in the game? Why didn't he bench him after three interceptions? McNair is awful. Shouldn't we go with O'Donnell?" one caller said.

The radio host replied, "I don't know if O'Donnell would have done any better because the Miami defense was blitzing so hard and the receivers were not getting open. So I don't know if it would have made a difference who the quarterback was."

Another radio caller disagreed, "I think Neil O'Donnell should be our quarterback. The team is just better with him. McNair threw three interceptions that led to 17 points. When are they going to get rid of him?"

The radio host responded, "Actually, the turnovers led to only three points."

Another fan said that McNair was only successful against the Rams because the defense caused three turnovers on their end of the field and the Titans only had a short distance to go. One fan even called in to say that the only reason McNair wasn't benched was because Coach Fisher would have been called a racist if he benched a Black quarterback for a White one.

Apparently, this caller did not know that Randall Cunningham was benched for a White quarterback (Jeff George); Warren Moon was benched for a White quarterback (Cody Carlson); Jeff Blake was benched for a White quarterback (Neil O'Donnell), and so on and so on. Nobody screamed racism at any of those coaches.

Jeff Fisher defended his decision to stick with McNair by saying, "Steve is our guy and Neil is the backup. It never crossed my mind to pull Steve."

Fisher said he thought that McNair's mobility would possibly put them in a position to get back into the game. That didn't happen because McNair had a bad game. So did the rest of his teammates that dropped passes and couldn't get open and gave up the deep passes on defense. So some of these Nashville so-called Titan fans were so busy hating McNair that they didn't watch the game.

"Quarterback Mark Brunell of Jacksonville is playing badly this season. In fact, his interception at the goal line with seconds to go is the main reason Jacksonville lost to the Titans. He wasn't benched. Instead, excuses were made about

Coach Tom Coughlin calling the plays and running back Fred Taylor being injured, so they don't have a running game," said one sportscaster in Nashville. "But they say Brunell will get it together and they will be fine. Not that these are not valid points, but nobody has made any excuses for Steve McNair's lack of a running game, decent receivers, bad play-calling, and recovery from a back injury."

So what's the difference between McNair and Brunell?

"Brett Favre's team is losing and he is throwing interceptions," said a former quarterback. "In Week 9, Favre threw four interceptions. In Week 7, he threw three interceptions. Favre wasn't benched. He wasn't booed. Excuses were made about his bad thumb that was injured in preseason. It's the same thumb that makes him a courageous hero, fighting through the pain to win. It's amazing how some Packer fans blame Favre's problems on Ray Rhodes (one of three Black coaches)."

On Thanksgiving, Thursday, 1999, against Dallas, Miami's Dan Marino threw five interceptions (two to Deion Sanders and two to linebacker Dexter Coakley), all of which led to Dallas Cowboys' scores. The first one came with the score 0-0. Marino threw the ball directly to Dexter Coakley, who ran it back for a score.

"Marino wasn't benched until there was only a minute left in the game. Then some of the sportswriters and fans made excuses about the pinched nerve in his neck and that being the reason he didn't have arm strength," said one sportswriter. Make no mistake about it, Dan Marino is a great player, but the problem is some of the sports commentators make him out to be perfect, while some other quarterbacks are flat-out ignored.

Drew Bledsoe threw ten interceptions and only four touchdowns from Week 10 to Week 13. During that time, the Patriots went from first place in their division to the middle of the pack.

There was never a negative word written or spoken about Drew Bledsoe, even though he wasn't performing.

Bledsoe was not benched. Again, the excuses were made about the Patriots not having a running game, and that was affecting Bledsoe. It's funny how that wasn't a factor when the team was winning. Just like Favre's thumb wasn't a factor when the Packers were winning and Marino's age or injuries were not a factor when his team was winning.

But nothing compares to the Trent Dilfer saga in Tampa Bay. During his time in Tampa, the Bucs had only one winning season. He had an amazing 70 straight starts before being benched in Week 8 of 1999. Erik Zier, the man he was benched for, later got hurt, and Dilfer was back in the lineup in Week 10.

In Week 11, McNair led the Titans to victory by rushing for two touchdowns in their 16-10 victory over division rival Pittsburgh Steelers. The next week, they lost to the Ravens after quarterback Tony Banks tossed four touchdowns and 41 points. A defense that had carried the Titans all season finally had a bad game. The lead receiver, Yancey Thigpen, was out again because of injury, and the other receiver, Kevin Dyson, had not performed that well.

"If they had a statistic for dropped passes, I would be the league leader," Dyson said. "I needed to step my game up when Yancey was not there. I didn't do that."

While his teammates were behind him, some people in Nashville constantly criticized Steve McNair, despite the fact the Titans were winning and on their way to the playoffs. McNair was booed again during the Titans 21-14 win over the Raiders after completing 12 of 20 passes for 114 yards. McNair told the media that he was bothered by the booing fans, but he understood that they had their opinion and it's tough to please everyone.

Those same people dogged Steve McNair because he had not thrown a touchdown pass in five straight games, yet they did not mention that he had rushed for seven scores. In the Titans' Week 14 win over the Oakland Raiders, McNair didn't throw or run for a score. He didn't need to; Eddie George rushed for three touchdowns and 200 yards. During that game, Randy Cross, a CBS sportscaster, said it was time for the Titans to make a change because McNair was ineffective.

Titans coach Jeff Fisher responded, "Randy Cross hasn't seen a game tape or seen a practice or been out here as long as I've been a head coach, so those kinds of things they say mean nothing to us. That's what they get paid for—to voice those kinds of opinions." Fisher also went on to say he would not get into hypothetical scenarios about benching Steve McNair. He said Steve was improving, doing what the team asked him to do, and most importantly, the Titans were winning. "There are a lot of quarterbacks that have ratings much higher than Steve that are playing on teams that don't have half as many wins as we do," said Fisher. "Steve has been our guy since we traded Chris Chandler away and there is no doubt about that."

Former Monday night football commentator Boomer Esiason told WNSR radio, "A lot of people around the country are wondering why Neil O'Donnell isn't playing. To be honest with you, they put so much money into Steve McNair, and maybe he will become that dynamic quarterback that they're hoping for, but you can't just live by handing the ball off to Eddie George. Neil is the perfect quarterback for that type of situation. The question is, what is Coach Jeff Fisher thinking about? My own personal feeling is that I liked the way Neil O'Donnell played and I would never have sat him down. Now that you have sat him down, it's going to be tough for him to get back to the level that he was playing earlier in the season. So I think you're stuck with Steve McNair."

Although I have never been a quarterback in the NFL like Boomer Esiason, I have watched every Titans game that McNair played in since 1999, and my opinion is not like his. Maybe

Coach Fisher is thinking about the same thing all of those Tampa Bay coaches were thinking when Trent Dilfer tossed all those interceptions for all those losing seasons. Or maybe he is thinking the same thing other coaches are thinking when they pick a starter and stick with him. Maybe Coach Fisher is thinking, "I am winning, McNair is performing, and I am sticking with my starter."

The McNair critics don't mention the fact that he missed five weeks for back surgery, he has yet to get a big play receiver, the turf toe, and numerous other injuries. Then, some members of the media are quick to pull up a statistical comparison between Steve McNair and his journeyman backup, Neil O'Donnell. Here are stats through Week 14, which were printed in the Tennessee newspaper sports section. The paper printed all these stats and a picture of Steve McNair with the headline talking about who should be the starter and how ineffective the passing game was. The irony is that the newspaper was quick to point out that McNair hadn't thrown a touchdown pass in five weeks, but they buried the fact that he rushed for a number of touchdowns and O'Donnell had rushed for none. Look at the statistics between the two players: Steve McNair—6 wins, 2 losses, 258 attempts, 140 complete passes for 1,565 yards (54%), 5 touchdown passes, 8 interceptions, and 7 rushing touchdowns. Neil O'Donnell—4 wins, 1 loss, 177 attempts, 107 complete passes for 1,236 yards (60%), 8 touchdown passes, 4 interceptions, and no rushing touchdowns.

In Week 15, McNair led the Titans to a playoff-clinching win over Atlanta, 30-17. McNair completed 15 of 29 passes for 219 yards, 1 touchdown (a 48-yard in their first possession), 78 yards rushing, and a rushing touchdown. During Week 16, McNair completed 23 of 33 passes for 291 yards and threw a career high 5 touchdowns and no interceptions as Tennessee beat the 12-1 Jacksonville Jaguars 41-17. McNair had two touchdowns in the first two possessions and three touchdowns in the first half. He was taken out of the game to rest at the end of the third quarter as some of the Tennessee fans cheered and clapped as backup Neil O'Donnell came in.

CBS analyst Randy Cross, who had criticized McNair and Fisher, apologized at half-time in the game, saying he was wrong about McNair and how "this guy can throw the ball and throw it well." ESPN analyst, Sterling Sharpe, said the following Sunday, "Hey, I was wrong about McNair hiding his arm with his legs. He proved that against Jacksonville."

In the regular season finale against the Pittsburgh Steelers in Pittsburgh, McNair completed 9 of 11 passes for 107 yards and one touchdown with no interceptions. In the team's opening drive, McNair tossed a 10-yard touchdown to tight end Frank Wychek. Because the playoff picture had already been set, McNair only played about a quarter before sitting out the rest of the game. His replacement, Neil O'Donnell, was instantly booed by Steelers fans, who remembered his playing days in the Steel City.

Here is a look at their season ending stats. McNair completed 187 of 331 (56%) passes for 2,179 yards, 12 touchdowns, 8 interceptions, and 8 rushing touchdowns, and 337 rushing yards. Neil O'Donnell completed 116 of 195 passes (59%) for 1,382 yards for 10 touchdowns, 5 interceptions, and no rushing touchdowns.

In the AFC playoff first round game against Buffalo, Coach Jeff Fisher said that he would not attack the number one rated Buffalo defense, and he didn't. The play-calling was the most conservative all season with very few passes going to the receivers. While McNair rushed for the team's first touchdown, nothing else was noteworthy of the offense. McNair passed for only a little more than 70 yards. Buffalo kicked what appeared to be the game-winning field goal with 16 seconds left.

With Tennessee trailing by four points and only 16 seconds on the clock, what was a sure win turned into a miracle—the

Music City miracle. Buffalo kicked it off to the right side of the field, and fullback Lorenzo Neal caught the ball then handed it to tight end Frank Wychek. He took a few steps right, then tossed a lateral pass all the way to the left side of the field to receiver Kevin Dyson. Dyson, with about five blockers in front of him, rushed all the way up the sideline to score the game-winning touchdown. The Titans won 22-16. McNair completed 13 of 24 passes for 76 yards and a one-yard touchdown run.

In the next game, Tennessee beat Peyton Manning and the Indianapolis Colts 19-16. The Titans trailed 9-6 at the half. In the third quarter, running back Eddie George rumbled up the middle of the field for a 68-yard touchdown to give Tennessee the lead. The Titans led 19-9 and were running out the clock when Eddie George fumbled. The Colts recovered and Payton Manning ran it in for the 15-yard score. Fortunately for the Titans, Yancey Thigpen recovered the onside kick, and the clock ran out on Peyton Manning. In that game, McNair completed 13 of 24 passes for 112 yards and 35 yards rushing. The numbers were modest and conservative, but they were winning.

In the AFC Championship, McNair led the team to a third consecutive victory over the division champs, Jacksonville. After trailing 14-10 at the half, McNair scrambled for a 51-yard run all the way down to the goal line. It was a key play in the game for McNair who was suffering from turf toe. McNair passed for just over 100 yards and rushed for over 90 yards. Their first score of the game was a McNair nine-yard pass to Yancey Thigpen. He also rushed for a one-yard touchdown in the third quarter and a one-yard run in the fourth quarter to ice the game with a score of 33-14. Steve McNair became only the second Black quarterback to lead his team to the Super Bowl against the St. Louis Rams in Atlanta Super Bowl XXXIV. The first, of course, was Washington quarterback Doug Williams. In Super Bowl XXXIV, the Titans lost at the last second 23-16.

McNair passed for 214 yards and rushed for a Super Bowl record (for quarterbacks), 64 yards.

"It's sad to come that close and come up short after playing such a great game," said McNair. "That's the bad part of this game. Someone has got to lose, but why couldn't it be a tie?"

The second half comeback would have been the first overtime Super Bowl in history. McNair led his team back from a 16-0 deficit. With 1:54 remaining in the game, Rams quarterback Kurt Warner threw a 73-yard pass to Isaac Bruce to give the team a 23-16 lead. In their final possession, McNair led Tennessee to an 88-yard drive, completing six passes for 48 yards and running twice for 14 yards.

On the final play, McNair was being chased by Rams defensive end Kevin Carter, the league's sack leader. He scrambled right, and Carter and Jay Williams grabbed him and appeared to have him sacked for a loss, but McNair stiff-armed the two, slipped away, and threw a 16-yard pass to receiver Kevin Dyson at the 10-yard line. During the play, ABC commentator Boomer Esiason got a little excited on the last play of the game when Steve McNair shook two Rams linemen and tossed a bullet pass to Kevin Dyson. Esiason shouted into the microphone for the entire world to hear as Kevin Carter and Jay Williams grabbed McNair, "WE GOT HIM! WE GOT HIM!" Had Esiason become biased and started cheering for the Rams? Or was he cheering against the Titans and McNair? Or was he doing both?

The Titans called their final time-out with six seconds left. On the next play, McNair threw a quick pass to receiver Kevin Dyson who was then tackled at the one-yard line, reaching for the goal line by Rams linebacker Mike Jones as the clock ran out.

"At the end, Steve made a phenomenal play to get the ball to Dyson and give us a chance to win," said tight end Frank Wychek.

"He's a warrior. He's a battler," said Rams defensive end Kevin Carter. "He's got such a big heart. He battled back and tried to win the game for his team."

"We did what we wanted to do," McNair said. "We wanted to have a chance to win in the fourth quarter. We just came up short."

McNair's teammate, offensive lineman Brad Hopkins, summed up the whole situation, "Steve McNair will never be judged fairly when compared to other quarterbacks. People can pretend it's not the case, but there is never a level playing field. The Steve McNair saga proves that."

Even at this point, there was still a double standard when it came to quarterbacks. Winning wasn't enough. Good performances were not enough; lack of talent was not an excuse. If you were a Black quarterback, from the time you took your first snap you were on the clock, it was only a matter of time before you made a mistake and got benched. The odds of you getting another shot after that were slim to none.

Let's take a look at some situations that actually played out this way starting with the bizarre treatment veteran **Detroit quarterback Charlie Batch got in 2001**. Batch had taken over the starting job as a rookie in 1998 because of injuries. At the time, he was considered the quarterback of the future. But playing with a bad franchise, bad coaches and injuries would eventually derail his career.

In the opening week, Batch completed 20 of 39 passes for 279 yards and two interceptions in a 28-6 loss to Green Bay. He was also sacked seven times. The next week, rookie coach Marty Mornhinweg benched Batch and decided to start journeyman Ty Detmer. The next week, Detmer threw seven interceptions in a 24-14 loss to Cleveland. He was one interception short of an NFL record. Detmer played the entire game and was never benched. He actually threw another interception, but that play was called back because of a penalty. The following play, Detmer threw interception number 7. Coach told the press afterward that he thought about pulling Detmer but changed his mind. The next week, Coach Mornhinweg decided to give

Detmer another chance because he said Detmer could play better. Why didn't he give Batch that same chance? Detmer started the next week and again performed miserably as he had for his entire career.

Detroit finally decided to go back to Batch the next week. Batch responded by throwing for a team record of 436 yards against Arizona in a loss (0-9). In spite of that performance, it was still evident that Mornhinweg and general manager Matt Millen had given up on Charlie Batch. At one point during the season, they started gradually putting rookie Mike McMahon into the game. With the Lions winless at 0-11, Batch separated his shoulder in the third quarter during a 13-10 loss to the Chicago Bears. That ended his season and turned out to be his last game with Detroit. For the rest of his career, Batch was a backup for his hometown Pittsburgh Steelers, playing in several games, but never recaptured the magic he initially had in Detroit.

In **1999, Ray Lucas(Rutgers)** became the starter for the New York Jets who were 1-6 when he took over. Lucas turned the season around and had a record of 6-2 as a starter. He completed 161 of 272 (59%) for 1,678 yards, 14 touchdown passes, and only 6 interceptions. The next season, he was back on the bench and not rewarded with a contract extension. In 2001 the Jets decided that Chad Pennington, the third quarterback, was their future. This was despite the fact that Lucas had played, performed, and won. Pennington, in his second year, had not started a game or seen significant playing time.

"I still don't think it's that widely accepted," says former Grambling star Mike Williams. "They have finally realized that I want to win football games and I need a quarterback that's mobile. I think those attitudes still remain."

After years of success in Philadelphia and revolutionizing the position, **Randall Cunningham** was benched in Philadelphia in 1994 and released in 1995. Not one team tried to sign him as a free agent backup. Some reports were out that it was his ego and attitude that scared teams away from the former MVP and all-time leading rusher among NFL quarterbacks. Yet other players with attitudes, egos, and a lot of other baggage were given several chances with several different teams to become starters—for example, former quarterback Jeff George. He was drafted by the then Baltimore Colts. He developed a reputation among teammates and coaches as a crybaby and headcase with a strong arm. When the coaches got tired of dealing with him, they cut him. He ended up signing with Atlanta. With Coach June Jones, the faces changed, but the Jeff George reputation and attitude were the same. This time it exploded as Coach Jones and George got into a verbal altercation on the sideline during a televised game. He was later cut.

He got yet another opportunity with Oakland, and again it was the same story. To this point, Jeff George had not led any team that he quarterbacked into the playoffs. He was eventually released again. He got another chance in Minnesota with Coach Dennis Green as backup to Randall Cunningham, who had won the MVP the previous year. The Vikings got off to a slow start with Cunningham with two wins and three losses. So at halftime of Game 6 and the team struggling, George replaced Cunningham. He started the remaining games and the Vikings got to the playoffs. It was the only time in Jeff's career that he was on a winning team and in the playoffs. The Vikings ultimately lost to the eventual Super Bowl Champion, St. Louis.

In the off season, the Vikings opted not to keep George. The free agent then moved on for another chance to back up Brad Johnson in Washington. Under a chaotic season where owner Daniel Snyder spent millions on veterans to supposedly win the Super Bowl, the team failed, didn't make the playoffs, and Coach Norve Turner was fired before the season ended. George replaced Johnson as the starter, but the results didn't change. In 2001 he was named starter for Washington and promptly led them to a horrible 0-3 start where they failed to score a single touchdown. George was finally cut and out of the league after three games in favor of Tony Banks.

Kerry Collins led Carolina to the NFC Championship as a rookie. Then a downward spiral started two years later as he was arrested for drunk driving, used a racial slur towards a Black teammate, and told his coach that he didn't have the fire to play football—basically quitting on his team during midseason. Carolina cut him. In spite of all his problems, the New Orleans Saints coach, Mike Ditka, signed Collins and made him a starter on a very bad New Orleans team. Collins failed. Then Collins got another opportunity when he was brought in with the Giants and Coach Jim Fossil. Eventually he took the job from Kent Graham. The team went to the Super Bowl in 2000. Collins had a miserable game against the Baltimore Ravens' powerhouse defense, led by defensive coordinator Marvin Lewis.

Remember Trent Dilfer when he was in Tampa Bay? In his first 39 starts he threw 39 interceptions and only 16 touchdowns. He started every game from 1995 to 1998. His performance didn't matter even with Tampa's constant struggles. In fact, look at the start of his career. Dilfer remained the permanent starter until he was injured with eight games to go in the 1999 season. He was replaced by Shaun King and not re-signed as a free agent. Dilfer then joined the Baltimore Ravens as a backup to **Tony Banks.** Banks had led Baltimore to a 5-3 record, but the only thing the sports media focused on was the fact that the offense wasn't scoring enough and Banks wasn't throwing for 300 yards every week. Eventually Dilfer replaced Banks. The offense didn't change. Dilfer didn't put up any better numbers, but that was okay. Baltimore went on to win the Super Bowl that year, crushing the New York Giants.

We watched Ryan Leaf, the number 2 draft pick in 1998 by the San Diego Chargers, blow up and scream at reporters in the locker room, act immature, almost get into a fist fight with a sports reporter, and string together terrible performance after terrible performance for a couple of years with the Chargers before he was cut. Nothing he did showed any signs of being a successful NFL quarterback. Yet when San Diego released him, Tampa signed him. He was soon released from that team and still got another chance with Dallas. In 25 games, including his stint with Dallas, Leaf had thrown 14 touchdowns and 36 interceptions. Now, how is this guy worthy of so many chances when other quarterbacks are not?

People were already criticizing Dallas quarterback **Quincy Carter** in his first year, saying that he could not play on the NFL level. This was after only a handful of games. How many rookies can you name that just came into the NFL and performed like a star in their first year? Sure, legendary Dan Marino tossed 20 touchdowns and only 6 interceptions his first year. Sure, he followed that up with a career high 48 touchdown passes in 1984. And in 2000, during his first year as a starter, Minnesota's **Daunte Culpepper** tossed 33 touchdowns and threw for over 3,900 yards. It is extremely rare for a rookie quarterback or first year starter (Culpepper) to come in and put up those numbers. While Peyton Manning threw for almost 4,000 yards and 26 touchdowns, he also threw an NFL high, 28 interceptions, as a rookie. Obviously nobody was giving up on him. Drew Bledsoe had 15 touchdowns and 15 interceptions his first year. He tossed 25 touchdowns and 27 interceptions his next season. The following season he had only 13 touchdowns and 16 interceptions. In fact, during his nine years in the pros, he has only had four seasons where he has had more touchdowns than interceptions. Nobody gave up on him. Ric Mirer threw 12 touchdowns and 17 interceptions in his rookie year in Seattle. He followed that up with 11 touchdowns and only 7 interceptions the next year. That is the only season he had more touchdowns than interceptions. In 1995, he had 13 touchdowns and 20 interceptions. In 1996, he had only 5 touchdowns with 12 interceptions, and in 1997 with Chicago 0 touchdowns and 6 interceptions. Nobody gave up on him. He is still in the league right now.

Then, there is Bobby Hoying. In his rookie year, he didn't really play and did not throw a touchdown. In his second year, he threw 11 touchdowns and 6 interceptions. That was the last year he would throw a touchdown pass in his seven NFL seasons. He threw 9 interceptions the next season with no touchdowns, but nobody gave up on him. He remained the number two quarterback in Oakland for three years until he was released in 2002. Even the great John Elway struggled early in his career. He threw only 7 touchdowns and 10 interceptions in his first year, but there was never any question about his future or if he was going to start no matter how he played or if the team won or not. There was no question he was the starter no matter who the coach was. He didn't win a Super Bowl until running back Terrell Davis came along in his last two years in the league. For all the talk about Doug Flutie, he hasn't exactly been a Hall of Fame player. In his first year with Chicago, he threw only 3 touchdowns and 2 interceptions. The next year he threw 1 touchdown and in his third year he threw 8 touchdowns and 10 interceptions with the Patriots. Flutie was released and had to go to the Canadian league to play. While the majority of quarterbacks who left the NFL for Canada did not get another shot to play in the NFL, Flutie did. The 5'10" quarterback returned to Buffalo in 1998. It was his best season as a pro. He threw a career best 20 touchdowns and 11 interceptions. Flutie followed that up with 19 touchdowns and 16 interceptions in 1999 and 8 touchdowns and 3 interceptions in 2000. In his first season with San Diego, he threw 15 touchdowns and 18 interceptions as the Chargers finished 5-11. The bottom line is that at 5'10", Flutie was not the prototypical quarterback. So why was he drafted and given a chance with Chicago and New England? Flutie was even given another chance after playing in Canada with Buffalo and San Diego. What's the difference between Flutie and Heisman winner Charlie Ward from Florida State? Again, Ward was taller, had better statistics passing and running, and played at a bigger program that went undefeated and won the national championship. But he was not even drafted.

The point is, in spite of some quarterbacks struggling on the field, they are given numerous chances to compete time and time again on different teams, but the window of opportunity for the Black quarterback has not been the same. The reason for the slow evolution of the Black quarterback can be linked to some NFL coaches who have been reluctant to name a Black quarterback the starter and let him develop over several seasons.

The strangest move was the Denver Broncos signing Arizona free agent Jake Plummer to a multi-million-dollar contract. He was deemed the starter by Coach Mike Shanahan. His track record was staggering. Four times during his career he threw 20 or more interceptions. At the same time, he never threw more than 20 touchdown passes in any season. He had talented receivers in David Boston, Frank Sanders, and tight end Freddie Jones.

As the face of the team and the field general, quarterbacks usually get most of the credit in victory and little of the blame when things go bad. The media has always selected a handful of great quarterbacks to make the poster child for the NFL. Players like Dan Marino, Tom Brady, Peyton Manning, Brett Favre, and John Elway served in that capacity. Each one deserved the praise for their performance.

Then there are the second-tier players who are liked by the press and given a pass even though their performance was not great but they get the benefit of the doubt and chance on top of chances. These are the up-and-coming guys or the players who got hot for a few games and suddenly they were deemed the next great thing. Even some mediocre quarterbacks fell into this category. All of the players in those categories often got a pass for poor performances. You would often hear phrases like, "he has no receivers or running game," "his offensive line is bad; they have got to do a better job of protecting him," "That's not his fault," or, "He needs better players around him." This is where the double standard comes into play. Black quarterbacks never get the benefit of the doubt on any level. On the other hand, comments from coaches, commentators, and the football experts the moment a Black quarterback has any kind of struggle sound a lot different: "he has got to learn to stay in the pocket," "it's time to put him on the bench for a while," "he is not getting it done anymore," "he has got to make better decisions," and "he is not the answer."

"Trust me, there are many White quarterbacks that are given plenty of chances and still are not getting it done," said Kordell Stewart.

"We are not satisfied being where we are. We are trying to take this further."

— *Shaun King*
quarterback 1999-2006

CHAPTER 8:

THE AUDIBLE

1999 TURNED OUT TO BE A PIVOTAL YEAR IN THE JOURNEY OF THE Black quarterback. There were several big time players who were having statistical success and winning at major college programs.

The NFL draft of 1999 was going to be the year that changed everything, the year of the Black quarterbacks.

Let's start with Syracuse quarterback Donavan McNabb, the second pick of the 1999 draft by the Philadelphia Eagles. At the time the Dolton, Illinois native had been drafted higher than any other Black quarterback in history. He had 49 consecutive starts in college and set the Big East conference record of 8,389 yards, 77 touchdowns, and an average of 221 offensive yards per game. He started every game during his career and finished with a 33-12 record. During his senior year McNabb led SU to an Orange Bowl berth over Florida. He finished fifth in Heisman voting as a senior.

The day he was drafted by Philadelphia, he was booed unmercifully by the crowd. What a way to start a career.

In his rookie season in 1999, he was a backup behind Doug Pederson, who was a career third-stringer. McNabb started the last six games and won two of four starts. He became the 27th Black quarterback to start in the NFL. In Game 10 he took over as the starter and led the Eagles to an upset 35-28 victory over Washington. The Eagles finished the season with a 5-11 record.

In 2000, McNabb was one of six Black quarterbacks to start on opening day. The Eagles beat Dallas 41-14. McNabb finished the season completing 330 of 569 passes for 3,365 yards (58%), 629 rush yards, and six rush touchdowns. He finished second to Rams running back Marshall Faulk in the league MVP voting. In the playoffs, McNabb led the Eagles to a win over Tampa, but they lost the next game to the New York Giants.

It was a memorable year for Donavan McNabb. Even though he accounted for 75% of the Eagles' offense, he was not elected to the Pro Bowl. Daunte Culpepper (Minnesota), Jeff Garcia (San Francisco), and Kurt Warner (St. Louis) represented the NFC. Kurt Warner ended up not playing because of lingering effects of a concussion. So McNabb made his first trip to the Pro Bowl as an alternate. The next year in 2001, McNabb led the team to an 11-5 record and a division title. He completed 285 of 493 passes (57%) for 3,233 yards, 25 touchdowns, and 12 interceptions. He also ran for 482 yards and 2 touchdowns. McNabb led the team to the conference championship before losing to the St. Louis Rams.

In 2002-2003, Donavan McNabb continued to be one of the best in the league. The highlight of the season came against Arizona when he broke his leg in the first half and came back to throw for over 400 yards and 4 touchdowns. Philly finished the season as division champs. In the NFC championship against Tampa Bay at home, the Eagles were drilled by a relentless Tampa Bay defense. Tampa won on the way to becoming dominant Super Bowl champions.

There was a Rush Limbaugh incident in October 2003. Rush Limbaugh resigned that night from ESPN's "Sunday NFL Countdown" three days after he made race-related comments about how the news media views the Philadelphia Eagles' quarterback Donovan McNabb. The remarks prompted demands for ESPN to fire Limbaugh the day before by Gen. Wesley K. Clark, a Democratic presidential contender, and Rep. Harold Ford Jr., Democrat of Tennessee, who said that he had enlisted 20 other House Democrats and had interest from three Republicans to sign a letter to ESPN protesting the radio commentator's comments. That Sunday, Limbaugh elaborated on his belief that McNabb was overrated and that the Eagles' defense had carried the team over the past few seasons.

"What we have here is a little social concern in the NFL," he said. "The media has been very desirous that a Black quarterback can do well—Black coaches and Black quarterbacks doing well. There is a little hope invested in McNabb, and he got a lot of credit for the performance of this team that he didn't deserve."

Two of the analysts on the show, Tom Jackson and Steve Young, commented on the football part of Limbaugh's remarks but did not address the racial content.

"My comments this past Sunday were directed at the media and were not racially motivated," Limbaugh said in a statement. "I offered an opinion. This opinion has caused discomfort for the crew, which I regret."

Limbaugh's departure ended a month-long experiment at ESPN in which the syndicated radio star—on a perch away from the other members of the show's main desk—offered essays about the National Football League and challenged the opinions of Jackson, Young, Michael Irvin, and host Chris Berman. Limbaugh refused to retreat from his comments about McNabb, saying on his radio talk show that the focus was on the news media, not McNabb.

Harold Ford, who was a representative in Tennessee at the time and is Black, said that he had no problem with Limbaugh voicing an opinion on McNabb's quarterbacking skills "but when he injected race and said the reason we root for him or that we have something invested in him is because he's African American is asinine. It borders on his motivation for making the comment beyond his assessment of Donovan McNabb as a quarterback. It suggests to me that he was thinking of things in cruel and nefarious ways."

During his time in Philly, McNabb led them to eight playoff appearances (2000-2004, 2006, 2008, 2009), 5 NFC Championships (2001, 2002, 2003, 2004, and 2008), and the Super Bowl. He threw for 3,875 yards and 31 touchdowns in 2004, the year they went to the Super Bowl.

After 11 seasons and 6 Pro Bowls, on April 5, 2010, McNabb was traded to division rival and chaotic Washington. This of course meant goodbye to Jason Campbell who had been in Washington since 2006. Keep in mind, during his last season in Philly he threw for 3,500 yards, 60% completion, they were 11-5 and in the playoffs. After getting off to a slow start on a pretty mediocre Washington team, things turned ugly in a game against Detroit. With the game within reach and Washington trailing by 6 with 1:50 left in the game, Shanahan benched McNabb in favor of journeyman Rex Grossman. Grossman came in and immediately fumbled the ball after being hit. Lions player Ndamukong Suh ran it back for a touchdown that sealed the 37-25 win for the Lions and highlighted the tensions brewing in the locker room between McNabb, Mike Shanahan, and his son Kyle, who happened to be offensive coordinator. Washington was 4-4 at this point.

"For him to be pulled like that, it's definitely a shocker to a lot of us," said cornerback DeAngelo Hall. "It does raise the interesting point, after the season, will he be here or not?" Then Coach Mike Shanahan and his offensive coordinator son

Kyle started spinning different stories about why they pulled McNabb. "The cardiovascular endurance that it takes to run a two minute, going all the way down with no timeouts, and calling plays, it's just not easy," Shanahan said. "If I thought it was the best situation to do, then Donovan would have run the two-minute offense."

Days later he said that McNabb was dealing with a hamstring injury, sore groin, and bruised shin and hadn't been able to practice the two-minute drill for five weeks. He claimed he discussed not playing McNabb that week. So why didn't he say that in the press conference after the loss to Detroit? He said he didn't want to really go into a lot of detail.

It's also important to note Rex Grossman played with Kyle in Houston the previous year, but never ran the two-minute offense in a regular season game because he was a backup who hardly played. Meanwhile fans were shocked and angered by the move the coach had made so early in the season that had clearly backfired. I interviewed fans at Velocity 5 in Virginia about the latest controversy with the Washington football team between Donavan McNabb and Coach Mike Shanahan.

"Basically, we got McNabb for one reason: that's to go to the playoffs. McNabb's a proven winner with five NFC championships. One Super Bowl, eight games, and six go down to the wire. He has been in the two-minute drill the previous games. The guy clearly knows how to run it," said the first fan.

"We are talking about the cardiovascular issue? The guy has been playing in the league for a number of years. I don't see a lot of cardiovascular issues with him. After rushing 45 yards, he didn't seem to have any then. I just don't think you bench a guy like that. He was rolling and throwing the ball well. I don't think that's something he should be doing," fan number 2 said.

When Coach Shanahan changed the story again to say McNabb had a hamstring injury, fan number 3 said, "The hamstring after the game Sunday? If he is having a hamstring issue, why is he standing up and not getting treatment? The guy knows how to play football, then you put a guy in there who gets kicked off the Bears team because he turned the ball over too much. What does he do? He turns the ball over and loses the game."

"I think it separates the locker room. Some defend McNabb, some defend Shanahan's decision. Ultimately if we are going to bring someone like McNabb here, a Pro Bowl caliber quarterback, you have to stick with him," another Washington fan recalled.

McNabb's agent Fletcher Smith was talking, even if McNabb wasn't. Smith released a statement saying Kyle Shanahan had been the biggest problem in the situation. "Their comments have been beyond disrespectful and unprecedented for a 6-time Pro Bowl quarterback such as Donovan. There have been many reports leaked of Donavan not being in shape and not being able to grasp Kyle's offense. The fact is Donavan came into camp in the best shape of his career having dropped 10 pounds in the off season in Washington working out with the team and never missed practice," Smith's statement read, "Unfortunately, it appears as though the Washington coaching staff decided that their 12-year veteran quarterback who flawlessly executed on the NFL's most complex offensive systems in Philadelphia is unable to grasp Kyle's offense. I believe there is tension between Donovan and Kyle that's rooted in the fact that Donovan has suggested modifications to Kyle's offense based on intricacies Donovan has learned in his NFL career."

After Donovan quickly led Washington down the field and scored what appeared to be the game-saving drive against Tampa Bay, Kyle was quoted saying, "he'll [McNabb] never take another snap for me again."

Shanahan responded with his own statement, "No one wanted him to be more successful than me. When the team was 5-8 and mathematically out of the playoffs, I made the decision to evaluate our other two quarterbacks. This was not personal but strictly professional. The decision was made in the best interest of Washington and I stand by my decision." During this disaster of a season that clearly wasn't working, Washington did something even more bizarre and signed McNabb to a long-term deal during the bye week.

> "I think they were too harsh on him and never gave him the benefit of the doubt. He was super successful there, but doesn't get his just do. In Washington, they undermined him and tried to act as if he wasn't smart enough to learn their offense after he had run Andy Reid's offense for double digit years. They played the typical games that are played against the Black QB."
> – Brian Mitchell, former Washington running back.

Washington finished the season 6-10. In the off season he was traded to Minnesota, where he only lasted a few games into the season on a bad team. He was released at the end of the season and never played again.

Shanahan would eventually say in a 2015 radio interview with ESPN 980 that he didn't want to give up draft picks for McNabb, but team president Bruce Allen orchestrated the deal. He said owner Dan Snyder is the guy who wanted McNabb most.

"He got a raw deal. Five NFC championships that took him to the Super Bowl. He had the city of Philly on his back. We don't know the truth about the Terrell Owens deal. He was saying one thing and now I was saying another; that's between them. But he got a raw deal there. Then he got a real deal; we went to Washington. It was almost like again they pushed him out of the lease, but all of the others got a chance to stay in. That is the narrative for black quarterbacks, a quarterback the entire time," says Akili Smith, who was drafted in 1999. **Akili Smith** had been a successful player on all levels going all the way back to high school. He says some schools wanted him to switch to another position, but he had no interest. "The first letter that I got from Oregon, they wanted to recruit me as a defensive back. I still have the letter. They want me to play defensive back even though I was one of the best quarterbacks in the nation. We played minor league baseball and then came back to football. My dad sent me a link in high school to continue to develop at the quarterback position." In junior college, Akili became the top quarterback in the nation. "When I went to Oregon, we had Dirk Cutter and then Jeff Tedford my second year. They simplified the game for me to understand."

After a successful run in college, Smith was the third pick in the first round by the Cincinnati Bengals. "Going through the entire process was an amazing blessing. Just getting that exposure so my family would have an opportunity to reap the rewards of everything they put into me when I was a child. It was just a great opportunity. The issue was the Bengals organization was not where it needed to be at that time. Marvin Lewis [Cincinnati coach 2003-2018] should be commended for a lot of things. I mean, he took the Bengals organization from the Stone Age into where the other 31 organizations were.

"My agent Lee Steinberg gave me a couple of options. He said to me, 'You're going to one of the worst organizations in football at that time.' You don't turn down a signing bonus like I got. Normally as a competitor you always feel like you can get things turned around. Hindsight is 2020."

During his rookie year in 1999, coach Bruce Coslet had Smith as a backup behind Jeff Blake. "Jeff Blake was a quarterback in Cincinnati when I got there. It was very competitive. Honestly, our relationship is better now than what it was in Cincinnati. We had a conversation and Jeff was like a man, I didn't know we couldn't have a great relationship in Cincinnati because they brought me in to replace him. So it was short-lived."

It was a bad start with a historically bad franchise. Smith went through a 27-day holdout, a decision he says he would later regret. "Now that I look back on it, I never should have held out. I should get my butt in camp. So when I got there, some players and coaches were feeling some kind of way to look at me. The next thing you know, the third game of the season and they just threw me into the fire after a holdout." From that point on, it was one thing after another that derailed any chance Smith had to succeed. "It's normal stuff for a rookie quarterback coming into the league. We had Darnay Scott [top receiver] go down in training camp. So that following year we took the field with Peter Warrick [Florida State] who we drafted in the first round. Ron Dugans from Florida State is well. Craig Yeast [Kentucky] was a second-year receiver. We had some of the veteran players mixing there. It was almost like we were a college team out there. Especially on offense."

Smith only lasted four games before a toe injury sidelined him the rest of the year. He was sacked almost five times a game when he did play. The team finished 4-12. Smith completed 80 of 153 passes for 805 yards, and threw only three touchdowns against nine interceptions. The next season, with Jeff Blake gone to New Orleans, Akili Smith was the full-time starter. It was the Bengals' first game at the new Paul Brown Stadium against state rival Cleveland. The Bengals lost 24-7. Smith only completed 15 of 43 passes for 250 yards, 1 touchdown, and 2 interceptions. He was sacked seven times. "I got beer cans thrown against me when I was playing against the Cleveland Browns. That's normal stuff. The N-word is normal."

Smith started the next four weeks, but Cincinnati lost every game. In Week 8, the Bengals beat Denver for their first win of the year, but Smith only completed two of nine passes for 34 yards before he was knocked out and replaced by Scott Mitchell. It was in the same game that running back Corey Dillon rushed for an NFL record of 278 yards. Smith would play in three more games before being benched for the rest of the year. At the end of the season, Smith had completed 118 of 267 passes for 1,253 yards (44%), three touchdowns, and six interceptions. In 2001, the Bengals' experiment with Akili Smith was just about over. He was demoted to third-string quarterback. He made his first appearance in Week 11, completing one of two passes for 18 yards in an 18-0 loss to Cleveland. In Week 14, he started his first game of the season, completing four of six passes for 35 yards before injuring his hamstring and leaving the game. He finished the rest of the season on the injured list. In the 2002 season, Akili Smith outplayed Jon Kitna in the preseason but he went into the season as the third quarterback. The Bengals started the season winless at 0-3. The two quarterbacks ahead of him did not perform well and ended up on the bench. Smith got to start the next game against one of the top defensive teams in the league, Tampa Bay. Behind a constant defensive blitz and a terrible offensive line, Smith completed 12 of 33 passes for 117 yards. He was constantly sacked. Tampa creamed the Bengals 35-7. He was benched and the next week replaced by Jon Kitna. Smith was furious and said he was going to ask for a trade in the off season. He felt like he would never even get a fair chance with the Bengals. As fast as the doors opened and slammed in his face, his playing days ended. He was released by the Bengals at the end of the year. "If you look back on my career, I made 17 in NFL starts in four years, 22 games, so that's equivalent to one season. By the end of my second year, I was benched because I was getting ready to trigger my incentives.I was not treated fairly in my opinion. There was never anything that showed me that I was the future of the organization."

Smith's next stop was Green Bay, a decision he says killed his career." I was listening to a new agent. I should've never gone there. I spent 30 days out there. Doug Peterson was quarterback coach. I was sitting in some quarterback meetings with Doug Peterson. He was bringing Brett Favre some breakfast and at that point I knew I was in trouble. They used to go hunting before the training camp meetings and that's when I knew I wasn't going to be there long." Smith says New Orleans actually offered him a two-year deal to backup Aaron Brooks before Green Bay. "I had a chance to play but I decided not to do it. I listened to my new agent, and that was the end of my career."

After being cut by Green Bay, his last shot and NFL roster spot was in Tampa Bay through NFL Europe. "Tampa was allocated through NFL Europe. I went to NFL Europe and had some success. I went back to the NFL to Tampa Bay and went to camp. The next thing you know Jon Gruden cut me. I had maybe one practice. I have no idea what happened there." Smith was cut before preseason. His NFL playing time was over.

"There is so much systemic racism in the NFL with the quarterback position. It makes absolutely no sense at all. Even if you say, we're not starters, there is no way you can tell me that we are not at least backups. We are not even backups in the NFL? We're talking about 32 teams . We are talking about maybe 90 players playing quarterback. So you're trying to tell me that the majority of the black athletes playing quarterback in college back in the day are the top 90 in the world and can't sit on an NFL bench. Even if I wasn't a starter in the NFL, you can't tell me that I couldn't have bounced around like Chase Daniels, AJ Feeley and some others. You can't tell me that."

After McNabb and Smith, **Daunte Culpepper (Central Florida 1999 1st round 11th pick Minnesota)** was Minnesota's future quarterback. He was 6'4", 255-pounds with blazing speed and a powerful arm. The Ocala, Florida native was an All-American who set an NCAA record for single-season completion percentage at .736, breaking a 15-year-old mark set by Steve Young (.713). He topped the 10,000-yard passing mark and the 1,000-yard rushing mark in his career, a feat equaled by only two others in NCAA history: Steve McNair and Doug Nussmeier.

When Vikings Coach & offensive guru Dennis Green drafted Daunte Culpepper instead of a defensive player, he was the subject of brutal media criticism. In 2000, starting quarterback Jeff George left to play for Washington as a backup. When his backup, Randall Cunningham (1998 MVP), refused a pay cut, he was cut and signed with Dallas. Coach Green tried to lure Dan Marino from Miami to Minnesota, but the future Hall of Famer declined, leaving Green with no choice but to name Daunte Culpepper his starter. The media scrutiny slammed Green even more."What was he thinking turning this team over to a guy who is obviously not ready to play?"

"We followed him very closely through college, and we knew he was a really talented player," Green said. "He's a quarterback's quarterback, a true field general. Aside from his ability to run and throw, that's what we really saw. He knew how to run a team."

All the football publications had the Vikings listed as last in the NFC Central Division with no possibility of making the playoffs. In Week 1 he was one of six Black quarterbacks to start on opening day of 2000. In his first game as a pro against Chicago, Minnesota won 30-27. Culpepper completed 13 of 23 passes for 190 yards and one interception and rushed for 73 yards and 3 rushing touchdowns. His 73 yards were the third most quarterback rushing yards in the team's 40-year history. (Tarkenton rushed 99 yards against the Rams in 1961 and Wade Wilson rushed 75 yards against Washington in 1987.)

"They made up their minds that they were going to stop Randy and Chris," Culpepper said. "I always like a challenge like that because I feel I'm a guy that can make plays."

"These young quarterbacks can beat you with their arms and their legs, and they showed that today," Bears Coach Dick Jauron said. Under Culpepper, Minnesota won the next three games. In Week 6, the Monday night showdown against Tampa Bay made football history. It was the first time two Black quarterbacks,

Culpepper and Tampa's Shaun King, had ever started against each other in a Monday night game. Culpepper completed 15 of 19 passes for 231 yards, two touchdowns, and one interception. After Tampa Bay's Keyshawn Johnson fumbled a pass on the Vikings' first offensive play, Daunte Culpepper scrambled for a 27-yard touchdown run, his fourth of the year. In the fourth quarter, Culpepper threw a 42-yard touchdown to Randy Moss, who jumped up and made a spectacular catch in double coverage.

"Everybody expected it to be intense, and it was," Culpepper said. "Everybody's going to be watching the big Monday Night Football game. We'd much rather be 5-0 instead of 4-1. We just came through. I don't care what people say about how we're not going to be any good. We are a good team. We keep proving that every week."

Minnesota won 30-23. "I'm not surprised at the success we've had. It's my first year starting, sure, but it's not my first year playing football. I know my own ability and I've got great players all around me. I don't think [teammates] ever really doubted me. Maybe a few did who hadn't seen me play. But I think I gained their respect in our first mini-camp by going out and showing them I was capable of handling this job." This game also featured two Black coaches on Monday night football. The battle featured Minnesota's Dennis Green and Tampa Bay's Tony Dungy.

"He's the biggest, strongest, fastest quarterback I've ever seen," said Bubby Brister, who at the time was Culpepper's backup. "I've never seen a quarterback with that much poise," former teammate linebacker Bryce Paup said. "A linebacker with an arm," said one defensive opponent.

Culpepper became the first first-round quarterback to win his first five starts since 1950. Under the passing of Culpepper, the Vikings won seven straight games. Culpepper finished the season leading the NFL in touchdown passes (33). He also completed 297 of 474 passes for 3,937 yards (62%), 33 touchdowns, and 16 interceptions. He was elected to his first Pro Bowl start.

In the playoffs, Minnesota defeated the Saints, but in the conference championship, they were blasted by the New York Giants 41-0. The Giants went on to lose Super Bowl XXXV to the Baltimore Ravens.

The next Black quarterback taken in the Class of 1999 draft was six foot 221-pound **Shaun King (Tulane 1999 2cnd round 50th pick Tampa)**. "Joe Gilliam and guys like Marlin Briscoe and James Harris...All the guys before us, they sacrificed, took some of the abuse that came with trying to play quarterback back in those days," said King. "We noticed what they did, and we understood. We greatly appreciate it, and we take it seriously the torch that they passed to us. We are not satisfied being where we are. We are trying to take this further, make it easier for the guys coming behind us."

As a senior in 1998, King led Tulane to an 11-0 season. He had an NCAA record of 36 touchdowns and only six interceptions (182.3 passing efficiency rating).

"I think you face obstacles in everything that you do. We have a better opportunity to go. Is it equal all the way? I am not sure. But I think if we continue to play well like we are doing, I think it will continue to get better."

As a rookie, King had more success than any of the other Black quarterbacks in the Class of 1999, even though it didn't come until late in the season. Initially, he started the season as an emergency third-string player behind Trent Dilfer and Erick Zier. When both of those players suffered late season injuries, King saw his first action in Week 12 against Seattle in the second half. He completed only three of seven passes for 32 yards and one touchdown in a 17-3 win over the Seattle Seahawks in Week 13, when he got his first career start. The next week, King completed 23 of 37 passes for 297 yards, two touchdowns, and one interception in the 23-16 win over the Detroit Lions. With the win, Tampa Bay was 9-4 and grabbed sole possession of first place in the Central Division.

When the starter Trent Dilfer came back, Coach Tony Dungy decided to stick with Shaun King, who had efficiently guided Tampa to the playoffs.

In the five games he started, King completed 61% of his passes and threw 7 touchdowns. King was able to lead Tampa Bay to the NFC championship game against the St. Louis Rams. It was the first time since 1979 that Tampa played for the conference title. Doug Williams, Tampa's first Black quarterback, unsuccessfully led the team against the Los Angeles Rams in 1979. Just like Williams, King also came up short in a 9-0 loss to the Rams.

The next year, expectations were high, and pressure was mounting. Experts were picking Tampa as Super Bowl favorites. King was now the full-time starter, so former starter Trent Dilfer was released and signed with Baltimore as a free agent. Tampa won their first three games.

King was efficient, but not spectacular. Coach Tony Dungy wanted his offense to be conservative and rely on his defense to shut down opponents. After starting 3 and 0, the Tampa ship started to fall apart. In Week 4 against the New York Jets, Tampa lost 21-17 after leading the entire game. They led 17-14 until Mike Alstott fumbled in the fourth quarter with 1:54 left in the game. The Jets scored the game winner when running back Curtis Martin tossed a pass to receiver Wayne Chrebet. On the very next possession, King was sacked and fumbled. Tampa would lose the next five games. They stopped a five-game skid after King completed 16 of 23 passes for 267 yards and four touchdowns in a 41-13 beating against Minnesota. The ship appeared to be back on track as Tampa finished the rest of the year 6-2.

One of the biggest games came in a Week 16 upset of the defending Super Bowl champion St. Louis Rams. King completed 18 of 38 passes for 256 yards, two touchdowns, and two interceptions. For the most part King was leading Tampa to conservative wins. Some fans and media began to blame King and the team's conservative coaching philosophy for the problems. Even some of Tampa's defensive players began to criticize the offensive game plan. Nevertheless, Tampa backed into the playoffs, but just as they had struggled during the season, Tampa struggled in the playoffs. Their Super Bowl hopes ended with a 21-3 loss to Donavan McNabb and the Philadelphia Eagles. During the regular season, fans, media and defensive players pointed the finger at the conservative nonproductive offense that only produced a field goal. King, who completed 17 of 31 passes for 171 yards, took much of the blame.

In the 2001 off season, Tampa signed journeyman Brad Johnson, who had lost his job to Jeff George in Washington. Dungy eventually named Johnson the starter before the season. King was demoted to backup. King would only play as a backup and start the final game of the season. Ironically, Brad Johnson did not fix Tampa's ineffective offense. It was still the same old conservative, ineffective offense with Johnson running the show. Eventually, Coach Tony Dungy was fired and replaced by John Gruden.

Brad Johnson completed 60% of his passes for 2,956 yards, with only 13 touchdowns and 11 interceptions. The difference is he was never blamed or benched because of poor offensive production. Under King, Tampa was 10-6. King completed 54% of his passes for 2,769 yards, 18 touchdowns, and 13 interceptions. So in three years, King went from NFC Championship starter, to playoff starter, to backup, to emergency third quarterback. He still has a career winning record and better stats than a lot of the starting quarterbacks at the time. Once he was released from Tampa, King ended up with the Arizona Cardinals.

"Race is definitely a huge role when it comes to development, patience, and opportunity for longevity," King says. "Black quarterbacks are not treated fairly. They are given one shot to make it, and if they don't excel, they are discarded a lot of time. That's why there are very few long-term backup Black quarterbacks."

The draft experts were high on Culpepper, Smith, and McNabb, and thought of King as a backup. Some of them thought the next player taken was destined to either play another position or go to the Canadian league. 6'4" **Aaron Brooks (Virginia 1999 4th round 131st pick Green Bay)** was drafted after Shaun King. During his rookie year, Brooks didn't play in any of the 16 games with the Packers.

The next year in 2000, he was slated to compete for a backup job behind Brett Favre with Matt Hasselbeck and Danny Wuerfull. To clear up the situation, the Packers traded him on July 31 to New Orleans to compete for a back-up job. He was listed as Jeff Blake's backup ahead of Jake Delhome. Saints Quarterback Coach Mike McCarthy, who was Brooks's coach in Green Bay, convinced Saints general manager Randy Mueller to swing a deal for Brooks. He made an uneventful first appearance against Chicago on October 10 when he rushed three times for negative two yards. He became the 31st full-time Black quarterback to play in the NFL. He came in again on November 5 against San Francisco, rushing two more times for no gain. Then in Week 12 against the Oakland Raiders, his career changed. Brooks came in during the second quarter, replacing Jeff Blake, who had broken his foot. His first pass was an interception, but in the next possession, he tossed his first touchdown pass, a 53-yard strike to Willie Jackson. The Saints lost 31-22. Brooks was impressive, completing 14 of 22 passes for 187 yards, 2 touchdowns, and 1 interception in his first real action as a pro.

Week 13 was Brooks's first career start against the St. Louis Rams. He led the underdog Saints to an upset win over the defending Super Bowl champs 31-24. He got the attention of everyone around the league by completing 17 of 29 passes for 190 yards, one touchdown, two interceptions, and 2 rushing touchdowns. The Brooks show continued in Week 14 against Denver, and he set a Saints record with 441 yards passing. He completed 30 of 48 passes for 2 touchdowns and 2 interceptions in a 38-23 loss.

Brooks helped the Saints clinch the NFC West title with a 23-7 win over the Atlanta Falcons. He completed 24 of 35 passes for 285 yards. Under Brooks, the Saints finished the season 10-6 and division champs. He finished the season completing 113 of 194 passes (58%) for 1,514 yards, 9 touchdowns, 6 interceptions and 2 rushing touchdowns. In the playoffs against the defending Super Bowl champion St. Louis Rams, Brooks completed 16 of 29 passes for 266 yards and 4 touchdowns (a Saints record) as they upset the Rams 28-31. That was his first playoff game and the Saints' first-ever playoff win. They lost the next game to the Minnesota Vikings, but Brooks had left his mark. He had done enough for the team coaches to name him the starter the next year over veteran Jeff Blake.

In 2001 with expectations high, the Saints finished with a disappointing 7-9 record. Brooks threw for 3,832 yards completing 312 of 558 passes with 26 touchdowns and 22 interceptions. He also had 358 yards rushing and 1 rushing touchdown. At the start of the 2002 season, Brooks missed the first part of training camp in a contract dispute. He pointed to the fact that he was one of the lowest paid players on the team with a $500,000 contract. It was his last year under the deal and Brooks wanted a raise and new contract. He quickly ended his holdout and returned to camp, but he was very unhappy that the Saints had not offered him a new deal. Brooks was released by the team after a few dismal seasons and ended up in an even worse situation. He joined the Oakland Raiders and only lasted a few games of the 2006 season. At the end of a horrible year, Brooks was cut and out of the NFL.

Michael Bishop (Kansas State 1999 7th round 227th pick New England) was expected to have a bright future in the league. He was a winner, strong-armed, mobile, and had played against top competition. He started at Blinn junior college before Kansas State. "Blinn College was a great experience. For the first time in my life, I was with some players that truly had the same passion as me. They wanted to win every play. We had an outstanding coaching staff that was not afraid to understand our culture and let us be who we are." Bishop recalls. The results brought two national championships to Blinn College.

After the successful run in junior college, Bishop was recruited to Kansas State where he continued his brilliance on the field.

"Kansas State and Coach Snyder gave me a chance to continue to play quarterback when other colleges wanted to change my position. Coach Snyder signed 14 juco players that he believed would impact the program. We came in starving with winning attitudes," Bishop says. "Honestly, I believe they did not have a plan for my talent at the time. For the first time in my career, I had to ask myself if I was too talented, too mobile, too strong, or too Black" Bishop did put Kansas State on the national map. The team was 11-1 his senior year and Bishop was runner up in Heisman trophy voting.

Once he got to the NFL, Bishop was mainly a backup with the New England Patriots. He had to compete with Drew Bledsoe and Tom Brady daily.

"Tom Brady was cool. We had plenty of conversation outside of football and shared our thoughts on current situations. The Pats never gave me the opportunity that I believe I should've had. Of course if you took a look at the quarterback room, I was the only Black quarterback, so it felt different. At times I felt left out of conversations. There were plenty of opportunities to be in the game when it wasn't going well for us, but Drew just signed a $100 million contract."

During his first exhibition game, Bishop rallied the Patriots from a 20-0 deficit against Washington. "This guy is a competitor," said starting quarterback Drew Bledsoe. "He's won a lot of games, and you can see why he is going to be around a while."

However, preseason winning and regular season winning were not the same. Bishop was inactive his entire rookie season. By the next season in 2000, Bishop was Drew Bledsoe's backup. He got a lot of attention with his performance in preseason but didn't see much playing time in the regular season. In Week 6 of the regular season, he entered his first game in the second quarter. On his first career pass, he tossed a 44-yard touchdown pass to receiver Tony Simmons. "It was a play we practiced all week," said Bishop. "The key was putting the ball up in the air as high as I could and hoping it got to the right guy."

He became the 32nd full-time Black quarterback to play in the NFL. In Week 7, Bishop saw mop-up duty in a 34-17 loss to the Jets. He completed two of six passes for 36 yards and his first interception. Bishop finished the season having completed three of nine passes for 80 yards (33%), one touchdown, and one interception.He spent the summer of 2001 in NFL Europe with the Frankfurt Galaxy. When he came back Bishop was waived by the Patriots before the last week of preseason. They decided to keep Tom Brady as the backup and the rest is history. Bishop was picked up by the Green Bay Packers but was cut a week later, and his career was over. Bishop got a late season workout with the Giants but didn't sign with the team. He eventually ended up in the Canadian League.

Bishop was the last Black quarterback taken in the 1999 draft. Rookie **Anthony Wright (South Carolina 1999 free agent)** managed to get a chance with numerous teams. The South Carolina player signed as a free agent with the Pittsburgh Steelers. While he did make the team as an emergency third quarterback, he was inactive for all games. Kordell Stewart was the starter. Mike Tomczac was the backup. The next season, Wright started the year as an emergency behind Kordell Stewart and Kent Graham and ahead of rookie Tee Martin. Coach Bill Cowher appeared to be high on Wright. However, he did not make the final cut and was replaced by rookie Tee Martin. On August 30, he signed with the Dallas Cowboys as a practice team player.

After Miami and Kansas City called the Cowboys and asked about Wright in late November, he was activated from the Dallas Cowboys' practice squad after rookie third-stringer Clint Stoerner was released. By Week 14, he played his first game as a backup against Tampa Bay. He completed his first career pass for 10 yards. The next game, with Randall Cunningham nursing a groin injury, Wright replaced Troy Aikman in the second quarter of the Washington game. Aikman was out because of a concussion. Wright completed only three of eight passes for 74 yards. The next game, Week 16, Wright made his first career start in a loss to the New York Giants. The following week, Wright started in a loss to the Tennessee Titans on Monday night football. Wright finished the season having completed 22 of 53 passes for 237 yards, no touchdowns, and one interception.

In 2001, Wright started the season as a backup behind rookie Quincy Carter. By Week 2, Carter was injured, and Wright made his first start of the season. The Cowboys lost 32-21 to San Diego. He completed 12 of 25 passes for 193 yards and tossed three touchdowns, three interceptions, and fumbled two times. The Cowboys would lose the next two games under Wright.

When Wright finally got a win the following week, it came at a cost. In a 9-7 win over Washington, he completed 15 of 28 passes for 177 yards, but was injured and missed the rest of the season. He started three of the five games he played in, and threw five touchdowns and five interceptions. It would be his last season with Dallas. September 1, 2002 Wright was cut as the team trimmed their roster to the mandated 53 players.

At this point in the NFL, 21 African American quarterbacks were active in the league. Wright ended up leaving Dallas and played with Baltimore, Cincinnati and in 2007 he left to play for the New York Giants.

"The Black quarterbacks and Black coaches have to be perfect. You don't get many opportunities to mess up."

— *Ja'Juan Seider*

2000 San Diego Chargers draft pick

CHAPTER 9:

INTERCEPTED

IN 2001 BLACK QUARTERBACKS REACHED ANOTHER MAJOR accomplishment. For the first time in NFL draft history, a Black quarterback was the top overall pick. **Michael Vick (Virginia Tech 2001 1ST round 1st Pick Atlanta) was drafted by the Atlanta Falcons.** He was considered raw by many draft experts because he only played two years at Virginia Tech. As a red-shirt freshman, he led the Hokies to the national championship game against Florida State in 1999. Even though his team lost, his strong arm and quick feet caught the attention of the NFL scouts quickly.

As a rookie, Michael Vick came off the bench in Week 1 and went 0-4 passing and rushed for 32 yards in limited action. In Week 2, he completed 2 of 2 passes for 27 yards and ran for 23 yards. He rushed for his first touchdown against Carolina in a 24-16 win but was injured on the play and missed the next week. Vick finished the season playing in 8 games, starting 2. He completed 50 of 113 passes (44%) for 785 yards, 2 touchdowns, and 2 interceptions. He also rushed for 289 yards and 1 touchdown. Year number one of the Vick era was a glimpse into the future for the Falcons. In 2002 the team cut veteran starter Chris Chandler and named Vick the starter. As the starter, he galvanized Atlanta, boosting ticket sales. He was one of the most popular players, with his jersey sales shooting through the roof.

Vick guided the Falcons to the NFC championship where they lost to Philly. Eventually, injuries, inconsistency, and a lack of any big play receivers stunted his growth as a passer. His career was derailed in 2007 when he pled guilty to dog fighting charges. "At the age of 21, I thought I knew it all," Vick recalled. "Who could tell me what to do at the age of 21, with all the money in the world? 'I am going to do what I want to do.' That was my way of thinking."

He was suspended indefinitely from the NFL. He was sentenced to 23 months in prison in 2007 and served 21 months. He was released by the Atlanta Falcons after being released from prison.

"I had money and a good team of lawyers and I thought things would work out for me. But that wasn't in God's plans," Vick said.

I talked to Mike Vick during an apology tour at the Covenant Baptist Church where he talked to members of the church. He walked into a standing ovation before discussing what happened. He was with then-president of the Humane Society Wayne Pacelle and Pastor Wiley.

"I used poor judgment. I had people around me who didn't have my best interest. I would fly home every week to go home and fight dogs... something so pointless. I should have been studying my craft, trying to be the best I could be. Instead, I involved myself in violence," Vick said. "It's a horrible thing and I wish I would have never done it, but I can't take back the hands of time."

Vick says growing up in Virginia, dogfighting was part of the culture.

He admitted that he never thought he would get caught. "Nobody wants to end up in prison, and you *will* go to prison for it," Vick said. "It doesn't matter who it comes from, me or the average person on the corner, it's all about getting the message out there, I think. When you know better, you're supposed to do better. I never thought about that until I got incarcerated."

Eventually after spending time in jail, he signed with Philadelphia, eventually replacing Donovan McNabb, then as a backup with the New York Jets and Pittsburgh.

At the start of the 2000 football season, there were 19 Black quarterbacks in the NFL. Of that 19, six were drafted in the class of 1999 and five were drafted in the class of 2000. On opening day there were five starters. The sixth starter, Charlie Batch, was injured but started the next week. The Bengals' Akili Smith was number seven because Cincinnati did not play in Week 1. Their first game was in Week 2. In Week 6 of the 2000 season, 12 Black quarterbacks played. Nine were starters. This included Ray Lucas of the Jets, who replaced an injured Vinnie Testaverde.

Ironically, being mobile had been something that Black quarterbacks had been doing for many years when it wasn't in vogue.

The Class of 2000 draft produced five more players who made NFL rosters.

Tee Martin (Tennessee 2000 5th round 161st pick Pittsburgh)

Martin had been a backup to Peyton Manning as a freshman in 1996. As a sophomore in 1997, he still didn't see much playing time, but in 1998, Martin had his official coming out party. He became the starter and led the Volunteers to a perfect season, culminating with a Rose Bowl win and a national title. He completed 153 of 267 passes for 2,164 yards, 19 touchdowns, and 6 interceptions and 7 rushing touchdowns. His senior year, in which he completed 165 of 305 passes for 2,317 yards and 9 rushing touchdowns, was not as spectacular since he played mostly with a bad throwing shoulder that he injured in the first quarter of the Florida vs. Tennessee game.

In his rookie year in the NFL, Martin eventually beat out second-year quarterback Anthony Wright for the third spot behind Kordell Stewart and Kent Graham. He did not see any regular season action. In 2001, he was initially Kordell Stewart's backup but was beaten out by free agent Tommy Maddox. Martin made the first appearance of his career in Week 17 during a 28-7 win over Cleveland. While he did not throw a pass, he did run one time for eight yards. In 2002, when Pittsburgh signed free agent quarterback Charlie Batch from Detroit as a backup, Martin was cut on September 1 as the team trimmed their roster to the mandatory number of 53.

He would end up as a backup for the Oakland Raiders and saw limited action during a Monday night game against the Green Bay Packers. It was the last stop for Martin, who would never play in the NFL again.

Spergon Wynn (South West Texas State, 6th round 138th pick Cleveland) was drafted after Tee Martin. Wynn started his college career at Minnesota before transferring to South West Texas.

During his 2000 rookie year with the Cleveland Browns, Wynn started the season as a third-string backup behind Tim Couch and Ty Detmer. He was elevated to starter after Tim Couch went down with an injury and Detmer tore his Achilles tendon during the season. In Week 4, Tim Couch was injured again, so Spergon Wynn saw his first regular season action. He came in at the end of a game where the Oakland Raiders whipped Cleveland 36-10. Wynn completed two of five passes for 15 yards. He got into the game again in Week 7 at the end of the game. Wynn completed two of five passes for 21 yards in a 44-10 loss to Denver. He completed one of three passes for two yards in Week 8 during the Browns' loss to the Steelers. In Week 9, as a backup to Doug Pederson, he came in at the end of the game and completed seven of 16 passes for 82 yards and one interception. He replaced an injured Doug Pederson in Week 12 for a few plays in the second quarter against Tennessee. He did not throw a pass, but ran one time for three yards in the loss. In Week 13, it was mop-up duty against Baltimore as he completed five of nine passes for 30 yards in a 44-7 loss. Wynn's first career start came in Week 14 against Jacksonville. He completed five of 16 passes for 17 yards, but was knocked out of the game and replaced by Doug Pederson. The Browns lost 48-0. It was a less than spectacular rookie campaign. Wynn finished the year completing 20 of 54 passes for 167 yards (40%), no touchdowns, and one interception.

After the 2000 season, Wynn spent the summer developing his game in NFL Europe with the Amsterdam Admirals. One week before the 2001 season, Wynn was traded along with running back Travis Prentiss to Minnesota. He started the last two games of the season after injuries to Daunte Culpepper and Todd Bouman. He threw the first touchdown pass of his career during this stretch. Unfortunately, he finished the season with six interceptions. In 2002, Wynn was released from Minnesota midway through the pre-season. He ended up in Canada and never played in the NFL again.

Ja'Juan Seider (Florida A&M sixth round, 205th pick San Diego Chargers) surprised a lot of experts when he got drafted.

One sports commentator said, "Why would they pick this guy in the sixth round? They could have gotten him as a free agent and drafted someone they might be able to get some use out of."

Another draft analyst said, "Maybe he can be developed into a receiver or defensive back. He is a bit of a project at quarterback. I think this pick was a bit of a stretch."

"I remember coming out. I went to West Virginia because they were playing Black quarterbacks; I would not have left the state of Florida. I remember being recruited by Florida and Notre Dame and Clemson a little bit. Growing up in my area, I wanted to go to Florida, but I knew if I went to Florida, I was going to a place of safety. Miami had a chance, but I saw what they did with Ryan Collins, and they were on probation. So back then it was so critical I thought I picked the school, but I knew I had an opportunity to play and wasn't caught up in all the BS."

The Belle Glade, Florida native was only a starter for one year. Seider transferred to Florida A&M University after three years at West Virginia.

"I was so thankful to play for Billy Joe at Florida A&M because he put me in a shotgun which allowed me to flourish and not be so mechanical when it comes to dropping back; I knew I had the arm and the speed. The size and the mentality to do it."

He was the first and only Florida A&M quarterback ever drafted as a quarterback.

"I mean it was difficult coming from Florida A&M anyway just because you're a Black quarterback. We only started one-year limited reps so it wasn't a lot on the resume. It's always hard. It takes one or two teams to like you. The interesting thing is, we made it to the playoffs so we got a chance for a lot of exposure. I think that the biggest difference was getting to the playoffs that year–beating Appalachian State, beating Troy State."

"We should have beaten Youngstown State, should've played in the championship, and I think that had a lot to do with helping me. Having a West Virginia background, they already had plans for me to come back with their grad assistant to work out there, so I got a little bit more exposure. More teams were coming out to see my ex-teammates who were going into the draft. Mark Bulger [who the Rams eventually picked] was coming out. They had to see two quarterbacks throw," he says. "I was fortunate enough San Diego brought their Quarterback Coach Johnson, and Bobby Beathard [general manager] was always known for going the small school route to find football players."

"I thought at that point we were in transition. It was okay to be a Black quarterback, but it still was hard because you have to be perfect; there's no difference in coaching. It's no different than coaching and coaching opportunities. The Black quarterbacks and Black coaches have to be perfect. You don't get many opportunities to mess up," Seider says. Seider says while Bobby Beathard was there with the Chargers, he was competing every day and right in the middle of it, getting a chance on the team. Then suddenly, Bobby Beathard retired right after the draft. Once he was gone, so were the opportunities. "A lot of it in the NFL is about being in the right place at the right time. At that time, San Diego was a bad place. We were still trying to see who the quarterback was going to be between Ryan Leaf, Jim Harbaugh, and Moses Moreno, and they had me, so they were trying to find out who was going to be the starter." Seider says San Diego was determined to give Ryan Leaf another chance even though he had been a bust at this point. For Seider, that meant limited reps in practice. "I thought I did well in practice, but I only got to play in one preseason game. I didn't have a lot of film. I know when I got let go guys were shocked. They couldn't believe it because I was actually doing good in practice." Seider says he remembers quarterback Marc Bulger getting released during preseason. He says the next week somebody had already signed him to their roster. "It was different back then. I think it's a lot better now, but it was different. I can't sit here and say it's not true but now I think the NFL has more spaces that can develop." Seider saw limited action during the preseason; he was cut before the regular season began. Seider went into coaching instead of playing in the NFL and is currently an assistant at Penn State.

Jarious Jackson (Notre Dame 7th round 214th pick Denver) was a two-year starter for the Fighting Irish. The

Tupelo, Mississippi native tore his knee ligament his junior year, but came back his senior year and started all 12 games. He finished with 17 touchdown passes and seven touchdowns rushing. In his rookie season, he played in his first game in Week 15 of the 2000 season. Jackson came in briefly for one play against the Kansas City Chiefs and threw one incomplete pass. It was his only appearance of the regular season. However, in the playoffs, with all the other quarterbacks hurt, he finished the game against the Baltimore Ravens, completing five of ten passes for 54 yards. Denver lost and Baltimore would eventually win the Super Bowl.

The following summer, Jackson spent time in NFL Europe with the Barcelona Dragons. When he returned to Denver for the 2001 season, he was listed as an emergency quarterback. He saw his first action of the season in Week 14 against Kansas City. Jackson replaced injured Gus Frerotte, who had replaced injured Brian Griese, and completed 7 of 12 passes for 73 yards. He was later cut September 1, 2003.

While the Jarious Jackson pick was not scrutinized much, he was considered a project that needed work. Besides, Jackson really had not wowed the college scouts with his stats. On the other hand, in spite of his small stature, Georgia Tech's Joe Hamilton did have the stats. His college career could not be overlooked. He was All ACC, All American, Heisman Trophy runner-up, Davey O'Brien Award winner for nation's top quarterback, and had completed 66 percent of his passes and thrown 29 passing touchdowns and six rushing touchdowns. Hamilton held school ACC records in total offense with 10,640 yards, 83 touchdowns total, and 65 passing touchdowns. To top that off, he was second in the nation in passing efficiency to Virginia Tech's Michael Vick. Joe Hamilton was taken in the seventh round with the 234th pick by Tampa Bay. The biggest question mark about him was not his play, but his height. At 5'10", Hamilton was small by NFL standards.

With tall odds stacked against him, Joe Hamilton managed to make Tampa's team as the fourth quarterback. He did not throw a pass in his rookie year. He played in one game and ran one time for negative two yards. Hamilton spent the summer of 2002 in NFL Europe working on his game. Unfortunately, he tore his knee ligament during one of the games and was done for the year. After being cut by Tampa, he ended up in Indianapolis but never got any playing time.

Quincy Carter (Georgia 2001 2nd round 53RD pick Dallas) was the third quarterback taken in the draft that year. Football experts said Quincy was not good enough to be an NFL quarterback and didn't understand why Dallas picked him so high. Carter eventually replaced Tony Banks as the starter. He started the first game of the season against Tampa Bay. Carter completed nine of 19 passes for 34 yards in a 10-6 loss. He missed the next two weeks due to injury. He came back against the Oakland Raiders and completed one of five passes for four yards before being injured in the loss. Carter injured his hamstring and missed several weeks. He returned in Week 12 to lead Dallas to a 20-14 win over Washington, completing 7 of 14 passes for 130 yards, 1 touchdown, and 1 interception. The Cowboys finished the season with only three wins, but felt they had a quarterback to build on. In Carter's injury-plagued first season, he completed 90 of 176 passes (51%) for 1,072 yards, 5 touchdowns, and 7 interceptions. He also rushed for 150 yards and 1 touchdown, but the critics from day one blasted the decision to draft Carter and blasted every move that he made on the field. In 2002, the Cowboys signed Chad Hutchison as a backup. It was strange because Hutchison had been playing minor league baseball and had not thrown a pass since his sophomore year at Stanford. But the 25-year-old rookie got a big contract to back up Carter. Behind a below average offensive line, Carter played inconsistently but decently. After a 9-6 loss to Arizona, Carter was benched and replaced by Chad Hutchison even though the team was 3-4. Seattle was not a strong team so Hutchison would have a fairly easy debut, furthering the case against Carter. In 2003, Bill Parcells was named the new coach. Carter led the team to a 10-6 record and a playoff appearance. He threw for over 3,000 yards, 17 touchdown passes, and 21 interceptions. He was the fifth quarterback in Dallas history to pass for more than 3,000 yards at the time.

In the 2004 offseason, Quincy was suddenly cut on August 4 of that year. There were suspicious circumstances around his release because he had previously failed two drug tests. He had started 31 games in Dallas. "He was smart. He understood it," Parcells said. "There he is, got his team to the playoffs, he's the starting quarterback of the Dallas Cowboys, he's playing well. I don't know all the problems or the demons exactly, but that's what eventually took him down."

In August 2004, Carter signed a one-year deal with the New York Jets as a backup. After Chad Pennington was injured, he ended up starting three games and winning two to help the Jets get into the playoffs. He completed 35 of 58 passes for 498 yards and 3 touchdowns. Carter was inactive for the playoff game against Pittsburgh because he was enrolled in a rehab program. That was his last season in the NFL.

While Vick and Carter made significant impact on the field, other NFL teams had African American quarterbacks on the roster as emergency players. **The Green Bay Packers signed Canadian football star Henry Burris (Saskatchewan of The Canadian League) in February.** He was released before the end of the season and in 2002 signed on with the Chicago Bears. He made the team as an emergency third quarterback. Henry Burris made his debut in Week 8 with the Chicago Bears. Burris completed 1 of 6 passes for 28 yards, 1 interception, and 19 rushing yards. Burris came in briefly against Minnesota after backup Chris Chandler was injured. He came in again in Week 13 for one play and tossed a 45-yard touchdown pass against the Green Bay Packers. In Week 16, he came in to replace an injured Chris Chandler against Carolina completing 8 of 22, no touchdowns, and 50 yards. Burris also started the last game of the season in a 15-0 defeat by Tampa Bay. He completed 7 of 19 for 78 yards and 4 interceptions.

Tory Woodberry (Winston-Salem free agent) signed as an emergency third quarterback and receiver with the New York Jets in 2001. He did not see any action at quarterback, but as a special team's player, he recovered a fumble against the Buffalo Bills in a 19-7 loss.

Quin Gray (Florida A&M 2003 free agent) made Jacksonville's roster as one of three Black quarterbacks. In 2005, Gray played in the last game against Tennessee, completing 14 passes for 100 yards and 2 touchdowns. The next season, he played in the last game against Kansas in the third quarter, completing 13-22 passes for 166 yards and rushing for 2 touchdowns. After injuries to the starter in October 2007, he became a starter for the first time. He went 2-1 as a starter. In 2008, he was with Kansas City when he came in during Week 11. He completed six straight passes with one being a touchdown to Dwayne Bowe. He also had a 27-yard run on that drive setting up the touchdowns. That was the highlight of his career. He was released in March 2009.

David Garrard (East Carolina 2001 4th round 108th pick, Jacksonville) made his rookie debut in Week 6 after Mark Brunell was knocked out with a concussion. David completed only 4 of 7 passes for 53 yards and 2 interceptions, but he rushed for 71 yards and 2 touchdowns. One score was a crucial 41-yard scramble to the end zone in the second half. David played for Jacksonville from 2002-2010, He played with the Miami Dolphins in 2012, before ending his career with the New York Jets in 2013.

Rohan Davey (LSU 2002 4TH round 117th pick, New England) saw his first action in Week 2 against the Jets, rushing two times for negative four yards. In the season opener of 2003, Rohan relieved starter Tom Brady (4 interceptions) as Buffalo stomped the Patriots. He completed 3 of 6 for 40 yards. He played with the Patriots from 2002-2004 and finished his career with Arizona in 2005. In his career Davey completed 8-19 passes for 88 yards with no touchdowns or interceptions.

Byron Leftwitch (Marshall 2003 1st round 7th pick, Jacksonville), was the second quarterback taken in 2003. He made his debut in the fourth quarter of Week 3 (September 21) against the Colts. Byron completed 4 of 5 and threw his first touchdown pass. After a short, injury-filled career, Leftwitch was cut in 2007 and signed with the Atlanta Falcons, the Steelers in 2008, Tampa in 2009. He returned to the Steelers again from 2010-2012 before going into coaching. He was the offensive coordinator for the 2021 Super Bowl champion Tampa Bay Bucs.

Seneca Wallace (Iowa State 2003 4th round 110th pick, Seattle) played for Seattle from 2003-2009. He joined Cleveland 2010-2012. Wallace was on New Orleans and San Francisco practice teams in 2013. He finished career in Green Bay in 2013. Wallace ended his career with 31 touchdowns passes 19 interceptions, and 4,947 yards.

Brad Banks (Iowa 2002) was a runner-up in the 2002 Heisman Trophy voting. In his senior season, Banks started all 13 games and threw 26 touchdowns and 7 interceptions. Iowa was 11-2 and tied with Ohio State for the conference championship. "My experience at Iowa was pretty good. I kept my head down and did the things that I was supposed to do."

Banks says after his huge success in Iowa, he got a serious reality check when it was time to go pro. Iowa was the number eight ranked team by the Associated Press. Banks won the O'Brien award as the nation's best quarterback. He completed 57% of his passes for 2,573 yards. He was Associated Press player of the year and Big 10 conference offensive player of the year. When it was time to go pro, NFL teams wanted him to switch positions. Banks says he was willing to change from quarterback to another spot for a chance to play.

"I want to let that be known, and I did so at the combine when I asked about it from reporters at a press conference. But as a Black quarterback you do run into those stereotypes like you can only be a runner, especially being six feet tall."

Banks signed as a free agent quarterback with Washington. They had drafted Gibran Hamden of Indiana in the seventh round. Hamden, a DC native, started only eight games in four years in the same conference where Banks played. Hamden threw for just over 2,000 yards, 9 touchdowns, and 14 interceptions on a bad Indiana team. So why did the team pick him? The scouting reports indicate they liked his strong arm and his 6'4" size.

"My experience in Washington was not fun. There was a lot of love from the fans and people in the DC area, but the experience in the Washington building wasn't good. Steve Spurrier was the coach at the time, and I thought that it would be okay to go there and play with him, being that he offered me a scholarship out of high school. Going in undrafted, you're not getting a ton of reps at practices. And when I did get reps, it would only be a few. One particular film session we would watch each quarterback's reps and when it came to my reps, being that we were pressed for time, Coach Spurrier fast-forwarded through them, and I thought that was bull crap," Banks recalled.

Banks was cut and replaced by Danny Wuerfel before the season started. "I know an NFL Hall of Famer, and he wanted to help me get back in the league after I was released from Washington. He had relationships with other coaches around the NFL. One coach asked him, 'Do you think he is smart enough to pick up the offense or can he pick up the offense?' And I thought that was crazy to ask being that I just played in a pro-style offense at Iowa in a very similar offense to what they ran at the time. So there is a stereotype for sure," Banks said.

Meanwhile, Drew Henson, who left Michigan to play in the minor leagues with the Yankees in 2001, was drafted by the Houston Texans. Henson had not even played quarterback in two years. For some reason, the NFL teams decided he was a hot commodity.

Marquel Blackwell (South Florida free agent, NY Jets) was an emergency quarterback after Chad Pennington broke his wrist in the third preseason game in 2003.

Vince Young (Texas 2006 1st round 3rd pick Tennessee) was runner-up to USC Reggie Bush in Heisman Trophy voting. He had been criticized for being a runner and an average passer with a side arm motion. Young was 30-2 in his career. He guided Texas to the national championship Rose Bowl win over USC in 2006. Young had 200 rushing yards, 267 passing yards, and 3 touchdowns including a 4th down 9-yard touchdown scramble) with 19 seconds left. They won 41-38. He was the first player in college football at the time to pass for 3,000 yards and rush for 1,000 yards in the same season, but when it was time for the draft, there were questions about his throwing motion and his Wonderlic test (test measuring ability to learn in the NFL). Long-time veteran Steve McNair had moved on to Baltimore. Coaches were rumored to favor drafting USC's Matt Leinart over Young, which would be a problem for Young during the start of his career. Somehow Young was still the top pick of the Tennessee Titans in the 2006 draft with the third pick. The 6'5" Young was named offensive rookie of the year and made it to the Pro Bowl in 2009.

He was a successful starter until 2008 when he injured his knee against Jacksonville. After being out 2-3 weeks, Coach Jeff Fisher named journeyman Kerry Collins the starter for the rest of the season. Tennessee finished 13-3. In 2009 Fisher stayed with Collins and said Young would have to earn his position back. Tennessee went 0-6, including a 59-0 beatdown by New England, before he changed back to Young as the starter. Coach

Fisher announced the change for his winless team saying, "I'm still in Kerry Collins' corner because I don't believe that our record is a reflection of the team play. I'm still in his corner, but we have decided to go ahead and make the change." Fisher clearly did not want Vince Young from the start but was forced to deal with him by General Manager Floyd Reese. Young won 8 of his 10 starts. He was named comeback player of the year.

By the end of the 2010 season, the feud with Fisher had exploded into the media and public. After a Week 11 injury against Washington, Young threw his pads into the crowd as he left the field, had a fight with Coach Fisher in the locker room, and stormed out. Fisher then named Rusty Smith the starter. In January of 2011, owner Bud Adams said Vince would no longer be on the team for the 2011-2012 season. He spent five years in Nashville constantly feuding with coach Jeff Fisher and was released July 28, 2011.

He eventually signed with Philadelphia but only lasted three starts in the 2011 season. After Philly, he would never play in a regular season game again. He bounced around to several practice squads in Buffalo, Green Bay, Cleveland, and the Canadian Football league.

Jason Campbell (Auburn 2005 1st round 25th pick Washington) led Auburn University to a Sugar Bowl win and was the game's MVP in 2005. The Laurel,Mississippi native was SEC offensive player of the year 2004. He was 2005 first round pick number 25 of Washington where he played from 2005-2009. He was traded to Oakland where he played from 2010-2011. Campbell signed as a free agent with Chicago in 2012 and Cleveland in 2013 where he started his first game Week 8 against Kansas City; they got beat 23-17. He snapped the eleven game losing streak the next week against Baltimore. He finished the season 1-7. He was released at the end of the season. He spent 2014 in Cincinnati as a backup to Andy Dalton and appeared in only four games before he retired.

In April 2015, Campbell declined offers from multiple teams to play football anymore. The Colts tried to get him to come back, but he declined.

Cleo Lemon from (Arkansas State 2001 free agent) was an undrafted free agent in 2001. The Greenwood, Mississippi native threw his first touchdown pass in 2006 as a backup. He also played in 2001 with Green Bay on the practice team. In 2002 Lemon was on the Baltimore practice team. He finished his career playing in San Diego (2003-2005), Miami (2005-2007) and Jacksonville (2008).

"I think today, with the lifespan of a coach, I think they truly will play the best player," said former quarterback James Harris. "Up until a few years ago, the problem wasn't the guys like Steve McNair, Warren Moon, Randall Cunningham, and Doug Williams. They were going to play. The problem was the backup guys. You didn't have any backups in a position to play. None of the guys who made the team were in a position to play. There are so many playing in college, you've gotten to the point where you see guys on the third team as quarterbacks. That's where it's changed. You got so many guys coming out of high school that colleges allow them to play quarterback; they don't have to switch positions. When I played, if you were going to a bigger school, chances are you were going to switch."

Former Denver Bronco Marlin Briscoe says the speed and size of the game has led to the revolution. "Defensive linemen are as fast as the wide receivers. The days when a quarterback can sit back with one option are gone. They need to be more mobile. You have got to have somebody athletic who can buy time if they can. Steve Young set the table. You see, all the African American quarterbacks that are in the league today have proven along the way that our assent to play the position is a correct one. Given the opportunity, we have done what we are supposed to do. The next hurdle we face as Black quarterbacks is not being called a Black quarterback, but just being called a quarterback, period."

"The NFL was the last bastion of the old White establishment, White boys club of owners that had come out of the original owners of the league," says former Philadelphia Quarterback Don McPherson. "You had a lot of these older owners who were much more conservative. Now you have guys who the bottom line is the TV contract. Guys who make the game exciting."

Doug Williams agrees that the bottom line is for players to be given the opportunity to succeed. "I think what has been given to these young guys today is an opportunity. Basically, that's all we ever asked for. An opportunity is no different in a work environment at IBM, Xerox, or being the lead reporter on the desk. Give us an opportunity and see that we can do the job. That's the bottom line."

"You face obstacles in everything that you do. We have a better opportunity to go. We get the opportunity. Is it equal all the way? I am not sure," says Tampa Bay's Shaun King. "I think if we continue to play well like we are doing, I think it will continue to get better."

Troy Smith (Ohio State 2007 6th round 174th pick, Baltimore) won the 2006 Heisman Trophy and guided his team to the national championship. He wasn't drafted until the 6th round by Baltimore. He played with Baltimore as a backup from 2007-2009. After being released by the Baltimore quarterback, **Troy Smith** signed with the San Francisco 49ers in September 2010. He was the 49ers first Black starting quarterback when he was named the starter October 27 against the Denver Broncos. He ran for a touchdown and threw for one in a 24-16 win. In that game, he completed 8-10 for 159 yards in the second half and led the team to three fourth quarter touchdown drives. His work got him named *Sports Illustrated* offensive player of the week. The next week, he led the Niners to a win over the Rams throwing for 356 yards, 1 touchdown pass, and 1 rushing touchdown. Smith started three more weeks while regular starter Alex Smith recovered from an injury. He was 3-2 as a starter vs Alex Smith's 3-8 record for that year. The Smith v. Smith drama came to a head in December. After Troy threw an interception and came to the bench, Singletary got in his face. Smith then got in his face in a heated exchange. After the game, Singletary said, "Troy is a passionate guy. The way he responded was fine. He's frustrated. I'm frustrated. We're both trying to get something to happen on the field." He was replaced in that game by Alex Smith. Despite a winning record as a starter, Head Coach Mike Singletary went back to Alex Smith. The spark Troy Smith had given the 49ers fizzled when Alex Smith returned as a starter. At the end of the year, Singletary was fired and new coach Jim Harbaugh had no interest in Troy Smith. No teams signed him.

Meanwhile, Alex Smith, who was the top overall pick in 2005, continued to struggle. Under Harbaugh, the team started to win games in 2011, but under Alex Smith they were 29th ranked out of 32 teams in total passing yards. They made the playoffs, beat New Orleans, and lost to the New York Giants. The Niners signed Alex Smith again for the 2012 season (3 years, 24 million). They were 6-2 when Smith got a concussion against the St. Louis Rams and was replaced by **Colin Kaepernick (Nevada).** The next week Kaepernick got the start as Smith recovered from injury. Colin completed 16-23 passes for 243 yards and 2 touchdowns in a win over Chicago. Kaepernick would remain the starter for the rest of the season, passing and rushing San Francisco to the Super Bowl (beaten by the Ravens). Alex Smith was traded to Kansas City the next season.

Here is the rub in the Troy Smith v. Alex Smith controversy. Why are some quarterbacks given chance after chance to play? They underperform and get more chances to play, but other quarterbacks like Troy Smith perform above average, then make one mistake and immediately get criticized, berated, and benched. Alex Smith had been the starter under Mike Nolan and was unsuccessful. He had been the starter under Mike

Singletary and was unsuccessful. But Singletary never got in his face even when there were plenty of chances for him to do so. Alex Smith threw picks and lost games for years, but in five weeks with Troy Smith, the coach was in his face when he had a 3-2 record.

Tavaris Jackson (Alabama State 2007 2cnd round Minnesota) also played for Seattle in 2011, Buffalo in 2012, and Seattle again from 2013-15.

Jamarcus Russell (LSU 2007 1st round 1st pick, Oakland) was 21-4 as LSU and was 2007 Sugar Bowl MVP. He was the top player with the Oakland Raiders. After three very bad seasons in Oakland with 18 touchdowns and 38 turnovers, he was released and wouldn't play again in the NFL.

Thadeus Lewis (2010 free agent Duke) had a long career as a backup and had few starts sprinkled here and there. He signed as a free agent with the St. Louis Rams in 2010 and Cleveland 2011-2012. He started his first game in 2012 against the Steelers, completing 22-32 for 204 yards, 1 touchdown, and 1 interception. He also played and threw passes with Buffalo in 2013. He was later signed and released by Houston 2014, Cleveland and Philadelphia 2015, San Francisco in 2016, and Baltimore in 2017.

Robert Griffin (Baylor 2012 1st round 2nd pick Washington) emerged as college football's best quarterback in his last year at Baylor. Washington traded several picks to move up to get the Heisman Trophy winner as the future starter. Initially Coach Mike Shanahan, who is known for flip-flopping his stories, praised the move. Years later after he was fired, he said the team gave up too much to get him. This marriage would play out in the first two seasons in the NFL.

Right out of the gate, RG3 secured his position as the starting quarterback over veteran journeyman and interception prone Rex Grossman. RG3's first pass as a pro was an 88-yard touchdown to Pierre Garcon. From that point on, the legend of

RG3 was born. There were no signs of being a rookie or a period for learning. Each week, the precision passing and scrambling got more exciting. The phenom was taking the league by storm. All of a sudden, a team that had been a bottom dweller in the NFC East had dug themselves out of the cellar and jumped on board the RG3 express. In 13 games, he completed 65% of his passes, threw 20 touchdowns, and only 5 interceptions. He rushed for more than 800 yards and 7 touchdowns that included an electrifying 76-yard run for a touchdown against Minnesota. The fans were chanting his name; the media loved him. The coaches couldn't get enough of the so-called "read option" style offense that NFL defenses could not seem to figure out. To those just watching highlights or the hard-core Washington fans, this was the perfect quarterback and the perfect system and the perfect time to start the Super Bowl chatter, not just for this season but for the next 10 years.

Everybody loved RG3 and could not wait for the next week to get more. The problem was RG3 often scrambled through busted plays, making something out of nothing look routine. His chaos and confusion were so smooth and worked so well that it looked planned. But it wasn't. Head Coach Mike Shanahan and his son, offensive coordinator Kyle Shanahan, were calling basic plays and letting RG3's athletic ability cover up for bad play calling. Another issue was RG3's inability to avoid big hits and to slide like the other quarterbacks in the NFL. Week after week, he would refuse to slide and get blasted by some defensive player. All because he would not go down or was trying to unnecessarily pick up one more yard by dancing on the sideline. Another factor was a bad offensive line that forced Griffin to scramble far too much or get sacked too often. "It doesn't matter how many times they hit me, I'm going to get back up," Griffin said in his press conference. "Even if they have to cart me off the field, I'm going to get off the cart and walk away."

In October, he was knocked out of a game against Atlanta after getting hit by Sean Weatherspoon. In Week 14 against Baltimore, RG3 injured his right knee when he was sacked by Haloti Ngata. In that same game, he injured his knee again after a 13-yard run. He limped around for several plays before being replaced by rookie Kirk Cousins. He missed the next game against Cleveland and finished the season limping on a bad leg against the Eagles. Washington won the division and secured a playoff home game against Russell Wilson and Seattle. Coach Mike Shanahan told the press RG3 was cleared to play, but renowned surgeon Dr. James Andrews said he did not clear him to return to play December 9. In the January game against Seattle, RG3 reinjured that same knee (LCL and ACL). So the drama in Washington had started. Who was telling the truth? Why did an injured RG3 even play? All those records set as a rookie–102.4 passer rating, highest touchdown to interception ratio–all pushed to the side by the now growing feud between quarterback and coach.

In 2012, RG3's knee problems continued. He played the season dealing with a torn ACL and LCL.

Going back to the 2015 ESPN 980 interview, Shanahan said several things about his time in Washington with RG3. About trading for RG3: "There were a lot of differences of opinion on which way we should go." He said he wouldn't have made the Robert Griffin trade if they knew about the salary cap penalties. "And if we do make the RG3 trade, we need to run the Baylor offense. We don't know if he's a pocket passer." He said he wasn't comfortable giving up the two extra first round picks and the extra second round picks because of the unknowns with RG3. He said he didn't do a good job teaching RG3 to slide and throw the ball away. He said there was a lack of communication with team doctor James Andrews giving the thumbs-up sign for RG3 to go back into the Baltimore game and injuring his knee, but Andrews never checked his knee. In another interview,

Shanahan said while everyone was celebrating RG3 being picked, he didn't think it was a very smart move to give up that much for 'a guy who we didn't even know if he could drop back and throw.' He said he sat down with the owner Dan Snyder and said, 'We can work with him, but we haven't seen anything on tape that warrants giving up this type of compensation.' To him it was absolutely crazy.

There is so much more, but this is a similar situation to what happened with McNabb. Shanahan was not a good coach and blamed the player, Bruce Allen, and the owner. His story once again was, "Here is another quarterback that I didn't really want, but the owner did." They were both Black quarterbacks to whom he questioned their mental capacity, their work ethic, and their reluctance to follow his and his son Kyle's commands without question. In both the McNabb and RG3 situations, Shanahan refused to actually make adjustments and do his job, so he failed miserably. He was later fired by Washington.

By 2013 the chaos in Washington had reached a new low with the team finishing the season at the bottom of the NFC east. The team was 3-10 when Shanahan decided to bench RG3 for the last three games in favor of Kirk Cousins because he was concerned about his health. "Anytime you've been hit as many times as he's been hit, I thought it was in his best interest, and the organization's, to talk about whether we should continue playing Robert if he's been hit as much as he's been hit."

Donovan McNabb didn't buy the Shanahan explanation. "This is about Mike Shanahan. Mike and Kyle Shanahan are trying to show why they feel like Kirk Cousins gives them the best chance of winning," McNabb said. "When you hear reporters that I know are linked to Mike Shanahan talk about RG3's preparation, you talk about he's missing some reads, you know, he's not reading some things. Everybody misses throws. What about the balls that are dropped? What about the offensive line not blocking? What about the defense not tackling anybody? He's coming off an ACL injury. But you wait 13, 14 weeks in the season to say, 'I want him to be healthy going into the offseason?' You might not even be there in the offseason." Donovan McNabb said Shanahan should look in the mirror and stop pointing fingers. "I'm used to this whole deal because, listen, I was benched for Rex Grossman. And he came out and said he gave the team the best chance of winning. Well, Rex Grossman finished the season 1-3; that didn't help nothing," McNabb said. "Sometimes you have to look in the mirror at yourself. Stop looking at everybody else. I don't think that he and Kyle Shanahan can do that."

The Shanahans were fired after 2013. Jay Gruden took over as head coach in 2014, but from the start had no interest in RG3 and wanted Kirk Cousins to be his guy. Receiver Santana Moss, who has openly criticized RG3, says Gruden ripped RG3 every chance he got.

By 2015, Robert had flamed out in Washington and had been picked up in Cleveland. He didn't take a snap that season. In 2016 he was voted team captain, but he was injured in the opening game and only played in five games. He helped the Browns win their only game of the season in Week 16.

The Baltimore Ravens signed him in 2018 as a backup. Robert later talked about his time in Washington as "being put in an impossible situation with a coach (Mike Shanahan) who never wanted me." RG3 says the story that he asked Shanahan to change to offense to pass more and run less because of his injuries was not true. Shanahan says the meeting did happen and went on to say RG3 thought he could throw like Aaron Rodgers.

Josh Johnson (University of San Diego 2008 5TH round, Tampa Bay) was the ultimate backup playing for Tampa 2008-11, San Francisco 2012, Cleveland 2012, Cincinnati 2013, New York Jets 2015, Indianapolis 2015, Buffalo 2015, Baltimore 2016, New York Giants 2016, Houston 2017, Oakland 2018, Washington 2018, and Detroit 2019. He won his first game as a starter with Washington in 2018 during his 11th season in the NFL. He had been signed during the season when the other quarterbacks – Alex Smith and Colt McCoy – were knocked out for the season.

Josh Freeman (Kansas State 2009 1st round 17th pick, Tampa) broke several records as a rookie in Tampa, including highest completion percentage in a single season, fewest interceptions in a single season (five), most consecutive seasons with 3000 yards passing (three), second most touchdowns in a career with 80. He was released partway through the fifth year with Tampa. Coach Gregg Schianno, who was later fired, benched Freeman in Week 3 of 2013. There was not only a growing rift between Freeman and the coach, but someone within the organization then leaked information about his medical records to the press as an excuse for his play and his release. He was released in October 2013. He signed with Minnesota in 2013. He started in Week 7. He was having concussion symptoms the next week and didn't play again that season. In December of 2015 he signed with Indianapolis. He started the last game of the season against Tennessee in January 2016. He was released in March. He retired in 2018.

Joe Webb (UAB 2010 6th round, Minnesota) played quarterback and several other positions in Minnesota. He also played for Carolina and Buffalo. He played both quarterback and receiver.

Tyrod Taylor (Virginia Tech 2011 6th round 180th pick Baltimore) played for Baltimore (2011-2014), Buffalo (2015-2017), Cleveland (2018), and LA (2019).

In 2017, while Buffalo was in the running for their first playoff appearance of the millennium, the Bills benched Pro Bowl quarterback Tyrod Taylor for a rookie. His replacement – Nathan Peterman, who is White – threw five interceptions in the first half in one of the worst quarterback performances in NFL history. Buffalo put Taylor back in and he led the team to their only playoff appearance of the 21st century at the time. In the offseason, the Bills traded Taylor and gave Peterman the starting quarterback job. Obviously that didn't work, but clearly this was a decision not made on performance or stats. There was something else at play. **"It's always going to be twice as bad just because of who I am–an African American quarterback," Taylor says.**

Dak Prescott (Mississippi State 2016 4th round pick Dallas) was supposed to be an emergency third quarterback behind Tony Romo.In Prescott's rookie season, Romo injured his back in preseason, backup Kellen Moore broke his right tibia, and Prescot was eventually named the starter and was 2016 rookie of the year. "I think the kid is coming into his own. Prescott doesn't get enough credit for how well he developed. Remember he was a spread guy coming out of college and he threw the ball well. He wasn't a great thrower, but he worked his tail off and now he's one of the better quarterbacks in the NFL. It isn't just on a quarterback to win all the games, quarterbacks need help to," Ja'Juan Seider says.

"*I see a bunch of average White quarterbacks that keep getting chances over and over again, while in the past the best Black quarterbacks got no respect.*"

– Michael Bishop

quarterback 1999-2000

CHAPTER 10:

FORWARD PROGRESS

IVEN THE FACT THAT THERE ARE SO MANY BLACK QUARTERBACKS playing in the NFL now and Black quarterback Patrick Mahomes won the 2020 Super Bowl, have we moved beyond these stereotypes about the Black quarterback's ability?

"I can sense that Black quarterbacks were more scrutinized, just as they are now. They were never given the benefit of doubt and were always questioned. I ultimately believe it's fear. I think they know if given an equal chance and level playing field, we would take over. Hell, look how many are successful now even when not getting the same chances," says Brian Mitchell.

Cam Newton (Auburn 2011 1st round 1st pick Carolina) was quarterback for Auburn in 2010 when they went undefeated and won the national championship. He won the Heisman Trophy the same year. He was the obvious best player in college and the clear choice as the top pick for Carolina. The owner of Carolina at the time, Jerry Richardson, did an interview with PBS broadcaster Charlie Rose about his meeting with Cam Newton before the draft.

"Newton was dressed perfectly," Richardson said. "I said, 'Do you have any tattoos?' He said, 'No, sir. I don't have any.' I said, 'Do you have any piercings?' He said, 'No, sir. I don't have any.' I said, 'We want to keep it that way. We want to keep no tattoos, no piercings, and I think you've got a very nice haircut."

Critics blasted Richardson comments calling them typical racial stereotypes that black quarterbacks continue to deal with.. Richardson owned the team when they brought in tight end Jeremy Shockey (who is White), who had more visible tattoos on his body than you can count. A football analyst at the time, John Gruden, had Cam on an ESPN quarterback segment where he would come up with a bunch of nonsense about if a quarterback would make it in the NFL based on his interview. He put Newton on the spot by asking him to spit out some verbiage from the Auburn football huddle. When Newton admitted they didn't call plays in the huddle, the critics pounced.

In his first season, he threw for 4,051 yards, 21 touchdowns, and 17 interceptions. He rushed for 14 touchdowns and over 700 yards. While he continued to improve until his injuries, the focus became more intense, not on his ability but on his character. He has been ripped constantly about his touchdown celebrations, flamboyant wardrobe, and postgame press conferences—even though other quarterbacks have the same antics.

Just look at the Patriots' former tight end Rob Gronkowski, who has brash celebrations, spiking the ball, taunting opponents, and making "69" jokes at his press conferences. Those things are brushed off as, "Oh, he's just having fun."

Cam Newton had reached the highest level of his pro career by 2015, becoming the first Black quarterback to win the NFL MVP award. The same year, Newton guided the 15-1 Panthers to Super Bowl 50 against Denver and Peyton Manning. Newton passed for 19-28 for 335 yards and 2 touchdowns with 47 rushing yards in the conference championship. They beat Arizona 49-15 to win the NFC championship. Super Bowl 50 ended in disaster for the 15-1 Panthers, who, up until this point, had the best offense in the NFL. Newton was sacked six times and Manning was sacked five times, both had two fumbles. Denver won 24-10. The next few years would be a nightmare for Newton, who had attained so much success in his career at this point. In 2016 the injuries started to build up, leading to a downward spiral. He only completed 52% of his passes, which was the worst of his career with only 19 touchdowns and 14 interceptions. Carolina went from 15-1 to 6-10. One of the tragic parts of this year was the number of unwarranted, unprotected hits he had taken while the officials refused to throw flags. It was clearly a blatant disregard for Newton's safety. For some reason, the officials would not penalize defensive players who roughed up Newton week after week. In 2017, he had shoulder surgery to repair a partially torn rotator cuff in his throwing shoulder. He finished with 3,302 yards passing, 22 touchdowns, and 16 interceptions and a career high 754 rushing yards and 6 touchdowns. They lost to New Orleans in the playoffs 31-26.

In 2018 Newton missed the last two games of the season and underwent right shoulder surgery. By Week 3 of 2019, Newton was diagnosed with a Lisfranc fracture and missed the rest of the season. The Panthers released him March 24, 2020. In June 2020, Newton signed a one-year contract with the New England Patriots. Immediately the media started with the narrative of "the attitude." Focusing on if his "personality" will fit the new team, his touchdown celebrations, and the way he dressed. How would the tough, stern, no-nonsense championship coach Bill Belichick deal with basically a running quarterback who was a loud-mouth, arrogant, malcontent? Keep in mind this was a week after signing the deal. That was insulting enough, but my question was how is a guy with this football resume not even approached by most teams as a free agent? Meanwhile, the

Colts went after 39-year-old Phillip Rivers who had never won anything significant.

"I got to know him pretty well coming out of college; training, helping him get ready for the NFL draft. He came into the league and had a really good career so far. Winning the league MVP in 2015, taking his team to the Super Bowl," says Hall of Fame quarterback Warren Moon. "He's been a little bit banged up the past couple of years. I think there are questions about if he is completely healthy or not."

"Cam Newton is in a situation where really the only thing stopping Cam is his injuries. The guy was an MVP; he led them to a Super Bowl. You don't just wake up like that every day and play that position," says former quarterback Ja'Juan Seider.

"What they don't like about him is in his interviews with the bracelets on the hats, receipt on the glasses of wine, going to the podium with your tight pants, overalls with no shirt on, some of it is self-inflicted." Akili Smith says.

Newton played 1 season with New England before being released. Eventually he returned to Carolina in 2022.

Colin Kaepernick (Nevada 2011 2cnd round pick San Francisco) replaced starter Alex Smith in his second year. Colin led the 49ers to the Super Bowl that season eventually losing to Baltimore. By 2016 Colin had turned his focus to something bigger than football. He wanted to bring attention to police brutality and racial injustice in America. He did that by silently protesting by kneeling during the National Anthem.

On August 26, 2016 in the 49ers vs. Packers game, Kaepernick sat on the bench during the anthem because the country oppresses Black people and people of color. He had previously not stood for the anthem, but now he was speaking out. The NFL says players are encouraged but not required to stand.

September 1, 2016, Kaepernick kneeled before the 49ers game against the Chargers and said he will donate a million dollars to organizations supporting him and the movement.

Then President Obama says Kaepernick has the right to protest because it's his constitutional right. NFL commissioner Roger Goodell says he doesn't agree with what Kaepernick was doing but supports players who seek change in society. Kaepernick had become the face of a new movement with several players joining the protest by kneeling.

While the majority of Black Americans were supportive of Kaepernick, some conservative white people were outraged at his silent protest and immediately turned this into a "disrespect the American flag" movement. The biggest objector to peaceful protest was President Donald Trump, who said Kaepernick and the other players should get out of the country if they don't like it, going as far as calling the protesters "son of a bitch" and saying they should all be fired.

Kaepernick responded, "He always says make America great again. Well, America has never been great for people of color. That's something that needs to be addressed."

He finished the season starting the remaining games that year ending with a loss 25-23 to Seattle on January 1, 2017.

By March 3, 2017, Kaepernick opted out of the final year of his 49ers contract and became a free agent. By the fall, a few teams expressed moderate interest in him, but none signed him. Many of his supporters say he was being blackballed from the NFL because of his kneeling in protest of police brutality. There were protests in support of Kaepernick outside the NFL offices in New York City, but nothing changed because Kaepernick was out of the league, a casualty of his cause. On October 15, 2017, he filed a grievance against NFL team owners, citing collusion to keep him out of the league. In April, the quarterback's representatives deposed Roger Goodell and a variety of owners with the exception of Dallas Cowboys owner Jerry Jones.

On May 23, 2018, NFL owners banned kneeling during the anthem, giving players the option to stay in the locker room.

This move made then-president Donald Trump happy. The owners soon retracted the rule because of its divisiveness.

Kaepernick had not only become the face of the police brutality cause and sacrificed his NFL career in his prime, but he had emerged as something bigger than just a football player. In September 2018, Nike made him the focal point of a campaign: "Believe in something, even if it means sacrificing everything. #Justdoit." While players were still kneeling during the anthem in protest, Kaepernick never got back on a pro football team.

By February 15, 2019, Kaepernick reached a settlement with the NFL on collusion, but the amount of the settlement was not disclosed.

On November 18, 2019, he got a workout with NFL teams, but it quickly went sideways because the teams refused to let the press in and refused to make it open to the public. So he moved the workout to a new location to have control over it and make it open. A limited number of teams came, but not one team signed him.

"We all know why. I came out there and showed it today in front of everybody. Stop running from the truth. Stop running from people."

Then George Floyd was murdered by a Minneapolis police officer (Derek Chauvin) who put him in cuffs, then put his knee on his neck for nearly nine minutes, Floyd yelling out, "I can't breathe!" until Chauvin choked him to death on video while several other officers stood by and did nothing. This led to nationwide protest and outrage all over the world. To his supporters, this was validation to Kaepernick's peaceful protest against police brutality. Many on social media began posting his kneeling pics all over Instagram, Twitter, and Facebook, saying, "America, if you have a problem with Colin kneeling, but you are okay with the officer kneeling on a Black man until he is dead, *you're* the problem. We have the right to fight back. Rest in power, George Floyd."

176

Several NFL players made a video urging the NFL to denounce racism (including Black quarterback and Super Bowl MVP Patrick Mahommes). So years after Kaepernick started a peaceful protest by kneeling against police brutality, June 5, 2020, NFL commissioner Roger Goodell put out a video saying they were wrong when it came to the kneeling protest that Kaepernick started. Goodell apologized to players for not listening to them. He encouraged peaceful protest and denounced racism.

"We the NFL condemn racism and the systemic oppression of Black people. We the NFL admit we were wrong for not listening to players earlier and encourage all to speak out and peacefully protest. We, the NFL, believe Black lives matter. #InspiredChange."

Then President Trump fired his criticism of the new attitude and support of peaceful protest: "Old Glory is to be revered, cherished, and flown high. We should be standing up straight and tall, ideally with a salute or hand on heart. There are other things you can protest, but not our great American flag. No kneeling."

"Kap is a baller! He stood his ground. Things are still happening daily, and that is why he kneeled," says Michael Bishop.

Russell Wilson (Wisconsin 2012 3rd round 12th pick Seattle) had a successful career at NC State before transferring to Wisconsin for his final season. The pro football scouts were still dismissive of his success and skills because of his height. They said he was too short and too small to be a good NFL quarterback. Once he got into training camp, everyone outside of Seattle was stunned when he took the starting spot from free agent Matt Flynn (who had just signed a big contract 3 years, $26 million). Wilson set a rookie record with 26 touchdown passes, and won Rookie of the Year. By 2014, Wilson led the Seahawks to a Super Bowl upset win over Peyton Manning and the Denver Broncos 43-8. He passed for 2 touchdowns and

206 yards. He was the second Black quarterback to win the Super Bowl.

"I want to see all these quarterbacks that are coming up because we have to do a better job of living the lifestyle. When we're in there, we get to live the lifestyle and take advantage of everything the NFL has to offer scores. Russell Wilson is a prime example of it. When I shot a Nike commercial with Russell Wilson, Grok, and Marcus Mariota, Sierra was there. Sierra is the mom of Russell. He had his own stylist with a Nike stylist. They were fixing his hair and making sure that everything was right. Russell is always positive, and he's always taking pictures with Aaron. He's living that lifestyle. That's what you have to do to stay in there, you have to live a lifestyle," says Akili Smith. "I take them out of your size, your height, your weight, and your color when you have certain traits like Russell Wilson. Russell Wilson has a lot of traits in him that allows him to be a winner. He's doing something, and I think that's the guy right now you can look at. Any quarterback in the league can say he's a guy doing that. Like that would be the guy I would look at, not even the home. And I will see how the hell is Russell Wilson winning games through and all these yards doing what he's doing at that size. Like that's the one I'm like, whoa! He may be the shortest quarterback in the NFL right now."

Dameyune Craig said, "I watch Russell Wilson play. I'm like, 'Man, that looks like me out there.' Russell can scan the field even on the run and he can make throws. He put a lot of pressure on the perimeter. You have to contain him. Like that was me in the flesh, but Russell's bodybuilding is a little different; he had bigger hands."

Jameis Winston (Florida State 2015 1st round 1st pick, Tampa Bay) won the Heisman Trophy as a freshman at Florida State. He also won the National Championship in 2014. He was the number 1 pick in the 2016 NFL draft by Tampa Bay.

"I was a coach at Florida State and when I was there, I put together both me and Coach Jimbo Fisher's list of quarterbacks to coach. I developed it myself. Jameis won a national championship and Heisman trophy for Florida State. A lot of stuff that goes into that position mentally: physical intelligence, leadership, toughness, ability to throw the ball with accuracy, the ability to win and lead. It's a lot of stuff that goes into that position," Dameyune Craig says. "I think Jameis Winston isn't in a good situation in Tampa.. What I mean by that is like when you have a franchise quarterback, that's who you build around. And I think when you're drafting, I think you need to be drafting offense of lineman. To protect him, you need a running back. I don't even know if they took a first-round lineman while he was there. I think he never got the talent around him," says Dameyune Craig. "I think he was a talent and never got the pieces around him to bring it out. So if you look at him, he's thrown together for the most yards of any quarterback in NFL history at his age and most touchdowns. He's doing things in the NFL that nobody's done before in the history of the game at a young age. I just think if you look at the way things were put in place around him, I think that hindered him. Hopefully he can mature. As soon as he fixes his decision making, he's going to be fine," says Akili Smith.

Deshaun Watson (Clemson 2017 1st round 12 pick, Houston Texans) won the national championship in 2016 at Clemson. Watson was in **the same draft with** Patrick Mahomes (10th pick) and Mitch Trubisky of North Carolina (second pick by Chicago). By 2019 he had led Houston to the AFC south title and a trip to the playoffs. They were 10-6 with Watson passing for 3,852 yards, 26 touchdowns, and 413 rushing yards and 7 touchdowns. They won the wildcard game in a come from behind win over Buffalo, but blew a 24-0 lead in the second quarter to Kansas City and Patrick Mahomes to end their season (final score 51-31).

In September 2018, Lynn Redden, the superintendent of a Texas school district, stepped down and apologized after he made racist comments about Houston Texans quarterback Deshaun Watson. Redden, who worked for the district for twelve years, in a public Facebook post after the Texans lost to Tennessee said, "That may have been the most inept quarterback decision I've seen in the NFL. When you need precision decision-making, you can't count on a Black quarterback."

Redden submitted his resignation letter to the Board of Trustees during a special meeting that was intended to discuss possible penalties for the educator. "I want to express my deepest apologies to the Board of Trustees, Staff, Students, and Patrons of the Onalaska Independent School District for the comments I made on Facebook," Redden said in his letter. "The comments were wrong and inappropriate and have been an embarrassment to the District, my family, friends, and to me." Houston Head Coach Bill O'Brien called Redden's remarks outdated, inaccurate, ignorant, idiotic statements. "I'll just let Deshaun's proven success on the field, his character off the field, speak for itself. He's one of the greatest guys I've ever coached. He represents everything that's right about football, about life," Coach said. "His teammates respect him, his coaching staff respects him, and in this day and age, it's just amazing that this BS exists. But it does. But we're moving forward."

Redden tried to defend his remark by saying that he didn't intend for the comment to be racist and was instead referring to the statistical success of African American NFL quarterbacks.

"Over the history of the NFL, they have had limited success," Redden said on Chron.com.

Lamar Jackson (Louisville 2018 1st round 32 pick Baltimore) was a dual threat playmaker in college who won the 2016 Heisman Trophy. Jackson was accurate with his passing and was a precision runner at the University of Louisville, yet some draft experts still doubted his ability to play quarterback in the pros. Former Indianapolis Colts team president Bill Polian and others said Jackson would never make it as an NFL quarterback and should move to wide receiver. Some interested teams asked him to run receiver drills at the scouting combine in case they wanted him to play that position instead. He refused to run the 40-yard dash so he could show his passing skills. Jackson slipped all the way until the final pick in the first round (32nd pick), at which the Ravens traded picks in order to select him—even though they'd passed on him earlier in the round.

"People forget Lamar Jackson was throwing for more than 3- to 4,000 yards a year and was coached in a pro-style offense in Louisville," Ja'Juan Seider says.

Jackson took over the starting role in Baltimore midway through his rookie season after filling in for injured quarterback Joe Flacco. The Ravens stuck with the rookie, who then led a relatively inexperienced squad to a division title. He was the youngest quarterback ever to do so at the time. A number of sports writers kept calling him a glorified running back after he struggled in the playoffs. In the 2019-20 season, his first full year as a starter, Lamar led Baltimore to the AFC north title. He set records for most rushing yards in a season by a quarterback and led the league with 36 touchdown passes. "Not bad for a running back!" Coach John Harbaugh would joke with the press during his post-game press conferences.

In December 2019, the San Francisco suspended radio analyst Tim Ryan for one game after Ryan referenced Jackson's skin color. "He's really good at that fake, Lamar Jackson, but when you consider his dark skin color with a dark football with a dark uniform, you could not see that thing. I mean, you literally could not see when he was in and out of the mesh point, and if you're a half step slow on him in terms of your vision, forget about it; he's out of the gate," Ryan said on KNBR's Murph and Mac.

Baltimore was one of the best teams in the NFL that year. Baltimore was defeated by Tennessee in the divisional round 28-12 and the playoff run was over.

"Some still don't think Lamar Jackson will last long because he runs a lot. He has the smarts and the accuracy of his arm in short to long throws. He keeps the defense on their toes at all times." says former defensive back John Booty.

Patrick Mahomes (Texas Tech 1st round 10th pick Kansas City) was drafted by Kansas City in the 2017 after a spectacular junior year at Texas Tech. He threw for over 5,000 yards and 53 touchdowns before deciding to turn pro. In his rookie year in Kansas City, he was the primary backup for Alex Smith. The next season Coach Andy Reid was so impressed with Mahomes, they decided to trade Alex Smith to Washington. In his first year as a starter Mahomes threw for over 5,000 yards and 50 touchdowns. He was NFL MVP and offensive player of the year. He joined Lamar Jackson (Baltimore), Cam Newton (Carolina), and Steve McNair (Tennessee) as black quarterbacks who won the MVP award.

"Patrick Mahomes is a straight-out freak of nature."says college coach and former Carolina quarterback Dameyune Craig. " The one thing he can do, target anywhere on the field, and he's accurate."

The next year, 2019-20, Mahomes led the Chiefs to their first Super Bowl win in 50 years by defeating the San Francisco 49ers. He threw for 286 yards and 2 touchdowns and rushed for 29 yards and 1 touchdown as Kansas City scored 21 straight points to come from behind and win.

"Mahomes and his baseball background shows he can make all kinds of throws, and he is not afraid to run and make plays," says former NFL defensive back John Booty.

Jacoby Brissett (North Carolina State) was drafted by New England in 2016. As a rookie, Brissett played in his first game September 18, 2016 in Week 2 against Miami because backup Jimmy Garoppolo had an injured shoulder. Brissett completed 6 of 9 passes for 92 yards in a 31-24 win. His first start was against Houston the next week, completing 11-19 passes for 103 yards and a 27-yard touchdown run in the 27-0 win. He was the first Black quarterback to start for New England. He injured his thumb in that game but started the next week in the 16-0 loss to Buffalo. Jacoby was an inactive backup to Tom Brady when New England beat Atlanta in the Superbowl. He was traded to Indianapolis in 2017 to back up Andrew Luck. He ended up starting 15 games because Luck was injured. He threw for over 3,000 yards and 13 touchdowns. He was back on the bench the next year, 2018, appearing in four games. Brissett became the starter in 2019 because Andrew Luck suddenly retired prior to the season. Indianapolis was a playoff contender at the start of the season until Jacoby got hurt and missed several games. They finished the season 3-6 and missed the postseason. He finished with 2,942 yards, 18 touchdowns, and 6 interceptions. In 2020, Indianapolis signed 38-year-old Chargers quarterback Phillip Rivers to be the starter over Brissett. "Jacoby proved his worth again and still gets a raw deal," says former New England quarterback Michael Bishop. "I'm a Charger fan. I've been watching Philip Rivers his whole life; Philip is done. They just hope Philip will come in and give them one season, to try to save some jobs. Jacoby Brissett should be the starter," says former quarterback Akili Smith.

Deshone Kizer (Notre Dame 2017 second round pick of Cleveland). had minor success playing for the Browns before playing briefly for Green Bay and Oakland.

Brett Hundley (UCLA 015 pick of Green Bay 5th round.) started nine games in 2017 after Aaron Rodgers injured his collarbone. He was a backup in Seattle in 2018 after being traded for a 6th round pick. In 2019 he signed a one-year deal with Arizona.

Kyler Murray (Oklahoma 2019 number 1 pick Arizona) made history because he was not only the Heisman Trophy winner, but he was the first player drafted in the first round by the NFL (Arizona) and Major League Baseball (Oakland). He was also the first quarterback ever taken as the top pick who was under 6 feet tall.

"Now you look at the league; there are a ton of Black quarterbacks going out there playing well, doing a great job, showing that they are very smart athletes. I don't care what color you are, you have to be extremely intelligent to understand the playbook; to be able to make those adjustments and changes," says Super Bowl champion receiver Gary Clark. "There are multiple ways you can try to win; you play to guys' strength. Let Lamar be Lamar; that's what makes them. They are supposed to let Patrick Mahomes be who he is. I hate when they say Black quarterbacks are scrambling because he can't read the defense. That's the thing about Steve McNair that drove me crazy. He took them to the Super Bowl; you think you got there because he couldn't read a defense? It's always a stereotype. So why is it a double standard?"

If you think it's just about winning at this point, look at two studies done by University of Colorado professor Patrick Ferrucci.

In 2017, the assistant professor in college media did an experiment on stereotypes specifically associated with Black and White quarterbacks. He asked people to rate the quarterbacks based on stereotypes and rate credibility.

The participants stereotyped White quarterbacks as more credible based on what he called the social identity theory. "We are all aware of the stereotypes that are out there in the discourse; it's almost unavoidable," says Patrick Ferrucci, co-author of both studies. "In these two studies, we were looking to see if people actually apply them, and the answer is yes."

Black athletes are usually lauded for their natural ability and strength while White athletes are praised for their intelligence and work ethic. According to the research, unconscious racial bias, sometimes encouraged by sports media, influences how the fans evaluate and view quarterbacks. It also factored into some Black athletes' decision to not play quarterback in high school and college. "If we're still stereotyping this way in sports, then it's probable that we're stereotyping in real life, too, and that could have far more negative consequences," Ferrucci says.

The first study had students of different races rate paragraphs and photos of Black or White quarterbacks on four stereotypical descriptors: strength, leadership, natural ability, and intelligence. All stereotyped the quarterbacks. The second study recorded impressions from only White people from a wide range of economic background, age, and education level. They assigned stereotypical descriptions to photos and paragraphs showing or describing Black quarterbacks but not the White quarterbacks. Even when told that a particular Black quarterback was extremely intelligent, the participants still didn't rate that player as being as intelligent as a similarly-described White quarterback.

"Everyone tries to lump all Black QBs together, but they aren't. Tom Brady is totally different from Rodgers and Tannehill–even Brees–and people don't try to lump them together, but they aren't as scrutinized as the Black QBs. I also feel that the narrative tries to use athleticism against the Black QBs, but **tries** to praise White quarterbacks for it [Fran Tarkenton, Aaron Rodgers, Steve Young, and Ryan Tannehill]. Tim Tebow was horrible, but look at the chance he got and the opportunity, despite being so bad," says retired NFL player Brian Mitchell.

Will we really get to a point where the skin color of a quarterback doesn't matter? That depends on who you ask.

"The current group is doing what we all knew they could do. When given the opportunity, we ball out. They are putting on for all of us that never got the shot. I truly hope they understand the magnitude of it! I see a bunch of average White quarterbacks that keep getting chances over and over again, while in the past the best Black quarterbacks got no respect. It will never change!" says former NFL quarterback Michael Bishop.

Some players think it's eventually coming because more Black players are in the quarterback position. Some say as long as the old establishment remains in positions of power, race will always be an issue.

"The only way that it's not going to be an issue is when they change the Rooney rule and start to demand some of these teams hire Blacks as head coach and general managers. There must be coaches, coordinators, and things of that nature if improvement is to be made." Akili Smith says. "When we start to get some Black people in those positions of authority and power,things will be different."

"College football gives the Black QB the chance to play," Brian Mitchell says. "So eventually they will be forced to stop the stereotypes because that'll be all they have to choose from."

Initially black athletes were not given a chance to get into the room. The doors slowly opened. A few came into the room, but there was no seat at the table. Through blood sweat and tears, they got a seat at the end of the table with no food. Now the black athletes want what they have fought to get for decades and earned. Not the crumbs and scraps. They want a level playing field so other black athletes can have an even better opportunity to be just as successful as anybody else who plays quarterback at the highest level.

ABOUT THE AUTHOR

WISDOM MARTIN IS A veteran television news journalist and anchor with more than 30 years of experience covering news and sports. He started out covering college football at Jackson and SEC sports in Mississippi before heading West to cover Fresno State basketball in Fresno, California. He later moved East to North Carolina where he covered University of North Carolina football and basketball. Later when he moved to Nashville, Tennessee, he continued to cover sports with his coverage of the Tennessee Titans Super Bowl. Wisdom later moved to Washington, D.C. where he covered the Washington Nationals and the World Series run of the Nationals, as well as Michael "Air" Jordan's last season with the Washington Wizards. Wisdom went on to cover George Mason University's basketball run to the final 4, Maryland Lady Terps championship run, as well as Washington's football team. During his career span Wisdom has covered a variety of news stories including Civil Rights issues with the arrest and conviction of Byron De La Beckwith, the convicted murderer of NAACP Field Secretary, Medgar Evers.

Connect with the Author

Website: wisdommartin.com
Facebook: wisdom martin
Twitter: @wisdomfox5
Instagram: wisdommartintveee